The GRANDMAS' Book

The GRANDMAS' Book

FOR THE GRANDMA WHO'S

Best AT Everything

by ALISON MALONEY

SCHOLASTIC INC.
New York   Toronto   London   Auckland
Sydney   Mexico City   New Delhi   Hong Kong

Library of Congress Cataloging-in-Publication data is available.

ISBN: 978-0-545-13398-2

First published in Great Britain in 2008 by
Michael O'Mara Books Limited
9 Lion Yard, Tremadoc Road
London SW4 7NQ
www.mombooks.com

12 11 10 9 8 7 6 5 4 3 2 1   10 11 12 13 14 15/0

Printed in the U.S.A.   23
First American edition, March 2010

To Mum, Dad, Kath, and Gerry – the best grandparents my children could have

NOTE TO READERS

The publisher and authors disclaim as far as is
legally permissible all liability for accidents
or injuries or loss that may occur as a result of
information or instructions given in this book.
Stay within the law and local rules, and be
considerate of other people.

To be the best at everything, you'll need to follow
common sense for the best interest
of your own health and safety.

Contents

Introduction	9
So Now You're a Grandma!	10
The Times They Have A-Changed	11
What Are Grandparents Made Of?	14
A Child-Friendly House	16
In Grandma's Kitchen	25
Glamorous Grandmas	31
Games to Play with the Grandkids	35
Growing Old Disgracefully	39
Don't Call Me Grandma!	42
Perfect Present Buying	43
Grandma's Lotions and Potions	50
It Never Did Us Any Harm . . .	54
Grandma's Arts and Crafts	56
Celebrities and Their Grandmothers	65
Grandma Green Thumb	69
Grandma's House of Fun	75
Crafty Advice	81
Grandmas in the Headlines	87
Out on the Town with Grandma	93

CONTENTS

Silver-Haired Stars of the Silver Screen   97

Health Warning   102

Story Time with Grandma   105

Some of the World's Greatest Grandmas   107

Teenagers Revisited   115

You Know You're a Grandma When ...   119

Long-Distance Grandma   120

The Other Woman   123

Grandma's Words of Wisdom   129

Household Tips   135

A Song for Grandma   138

It's Never Too Late To ...   139

The Joke's on Grandma   140

Introduction

So, after raising your own children and sitting back for a few years while they make their own way in the world, you receive the delightful news that you're going to become a grandmother. Suddenly you're surrounded by diapers and screaming babies, and the house is full of kids and toys again.

Of course, you take it all in stride. Having done it all before with your own family, you can quickly switch back into superwoman mode without a problem.

The grandma who's best at everything thinks nothing of rushing home from work to babysit her adorable grandchildren while their stressed mother has a well-earned night out. She's always on the end of the phone when advice is needed, and she's there in a flash when there's a family crisis.

She can tell you how to get grape juice stains out of baby's best white T-shirt, and she always knows the best way to get the kids to sleep. Who else can a worried mom turn to when she is juggling work and children and needs a helping hand?

For some grandmas, though, much may have changed since their motherhood days, so this quick refresher course may be just the thing to pick up a few new child-care tips, find out the best babysitting activities, and learn how to deal with the other grandma in your grandchild's life.

But never forget that to your grandchildren, you will always be the best at everything.

So Now You're a Grandma!

You'll never forget that magical moment when you first find out you're going to become a grandma. As soon as the joyful news has sunk in, your life changes. You'll be bursting with excitement, and before you know it, you'll start buying baby clothes and dishing out advice.

But before you get carried away, stop and take a deep breath.

The hardest thing for a grandma to do is to remember to take a step back and wait to be asked for any help. Although a little gentle guidance may be needed occasionally, it's never wise to undermine the confidence of a new mom or dad by jumping in and being overly critical. Most new moms will appreciate well-meaning words of wisdom offered by a parent or mother-in-law, but only up to a point.

The golden rule is *listen to yourself*. If you realize you're starting every sentence with "You should be . . ." or "Why are you . . . ," then you're heading for trouble!

"A mother becomes a true grandmother the day she stops noticing the terrible things her children do because she is so enchanted with the wonderful things her grandchildren do."
LOIS WYSE, author

The Times They Have A-Changed

(or Things You Shouldn't Say to the Parents of Your Grandchild)

Shouldn't the baby be out of diapers by now?

This question is a classic mistake most grandmas seem unable to avoid, but it's one that is guaranteed to annoy your grandchild's parents. Expert advice now leans toward later potty training, and as long as the child is not nearing school age, the decision should be left to Mom and Dad. After all, they're the ones who have to deal with the "accidents"!

Make sure the baby is wrapped up warmly.

This is good advice before an outdoor trip in January, but it's not necessarily good advice if the baby is being put to bed in a centrally heated house. Overheating a baby can contribute to Sudden Infant Death Syndrome (SIDS). The temperature of the nursery should be around 68°F, and wrapping a baby too tightly in blankets can be dangerous. It's also important that the baby's head remains uncovered.

The baby shouldn't have a pacifier at this age.

A pacifier wedged firmly in the mouth of a five-year-old is not a good look, but it won't actually do any harm. And research has shown that in young babies, a pacifier at bedtime can help to prevent SIDS.

Shouldn't the baby be lying facedown?

For many grandmas, this is a tough one. When your children were young, the advice was to lay babies on their stomachs. However, in the early 1990s, the "Back to Sleep" campaign changed things. It was discovered that babies sleeping on their backs were much less likely to die from SIDS, and since the change in advice, the number of SIDS victims has fallen by more than 50 percent.

Shouldn't the baby be eating solid foods by now?

Weaning used to start at four months, but World Health Organization guidelines now state that it shouldn't begin until the child is six months old. Experts believe that children are healthier if their sole source of nutrition for the first six months is breast milk, although bottled milk is the next best thing.

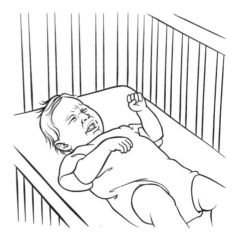

You can't leave the baby crying in the crib!

As difficult as it is to hear your beloved grandchild sobbing at bedtime, many modern parents use the "controlled crying" technique for children over six months of age. It takes a lot of willpower, but it really can work. Unless the child is genuinely frightened or hysterical, he or she can be left to cry slightly longer each time, starting at around five minutes. If you go in after that time, stroking and patting is better than lifting and cuddling. All that difficult work will be quickly undone if Grandma runs in and gives baby a hug every time he or she whimpers!

Shouldn't the baby be in bed by now?

Not everybody believes a rigid routine at bedtime is necessary. While many parents insist on tucking in their little darlings by 7 p.m., it is perfectly acceptable for others to put them to bed whenever they feel the time is right. In fact, for working parents, quality time with their children in the evenings is more important than an inflexible routine.

You won't be going back to work, I hope?

Depending on your age, you may have raised your children when the majority of mothers stayed at home. Things are very different today. Some women prefer to go back to work, while others opt to become full-time moms. And the reality of modern life is that many mothers work because they have to.

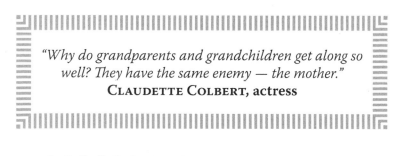

"Why do grandparents and grandchildren get along so well? They have the same enemy — the mother."
CLAUDETTE COLBERT, actress

What Are Grandparents Made Of?

Grandparents today are younger, healthier, and more active than ever before. Here are some fascinating facts and figures.

∗ There are around 56 million grandparents in the United States, of which 5.7 million have their grandchildren under age eighteen living with them.

∗ On average, people spend at least one year with a child still living at home while they are also a grandparent.

∗ One in two grandparents has a living parent.

∗ Nearly one-third of people aged fifty and over are grandparents.

∗ The average age when people become grandparents is just forty-seven years.

∗ By the age of fifty-four, one in every two people is a grandparent.

∗ More than a third of grandparents spend the equivalent of three days a week caring for their grandchildren.

∗ In the United States, 28 percent of preschool children with employed mothers are cared for by their grandparents while their mothers work.

✳ 1.4 million grandparents in the United States are both working and looking after the basic needs of their grandchildren.

A Child-Friendly House

It's been a while since you had your own children, and while a quick glance around your house might tell you it's a perfectly safe environment, your son or daughter is guaranteed to disagree. Small children seem to be attracted to any dangers around them, especially at that crawling, curious stage when they want to investigate the contents of every cabinet and pull everything they can reach down to their level.

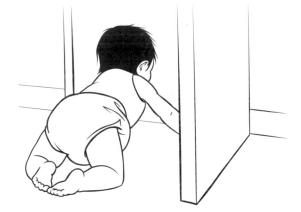

Here are some guidelines to help make your house safer for visiting grandchildren.

* Medicines, cleaning fluids, alcohol, and vitamins MUST be locked away in a cabinet that is completely out of children's reach. It takes a split second for a toddler to find a bottle of medicine or bleach, and the consequences could be disastrous.

✳ When using the stove, put pans on the rear burners, with the handles turned back. Make sure your kettle is at the back of your work surface and out of grabbing distance.

✳ Put child locks on kitchen cabinets, especially those containing glass or ceramics.

✳ Never keep glasses on a tray on top of a table. A toddler can easily reach up and pull the tray down on top of her- or himself. Move anything accessible to a higher shelf.

✳ Never leave an iron on near a child, even if you are just turning around for a second.

✳ As soon as the child starts to crawl, gates to block the stairs are a must.

✳ Make sure that young children can't open your front door. A bright three-year-old can use a key or find a chair to stand on to undo the latch. He or she will be out in the yard or street before you realize it.

✳ Open windows only at the top, and never open them wide enough for a child to crawl out. Lock the larger windows and make sure that open windows are not accessible by climbing on beds, sofas, or other furniture.

"A house needs a grandma in it."
LOUISA MAY ALCOTT, author

Babysitting Hazards

✳ As the only adult left in the house, you are expected to play endless games of Go Fish.

✳ Babies are happy to play peekaboo for hours!

✳ The minute the parents leave the house, the children will swear that Mom said they could stay up late/eat chocolate/watch a DVD.

✳ When you've finally gotten the kids to bed, there will be nothing you want to watch on TV and you'll wish they were still up.

✳ "I promise we'll be back by midnight" means you'll be lucky to see the parents before 2 a.m.

✳ You will spend half the night reading "just one more" bedtime story.

The Little White Lies
(and what really happened)

✳ "They ate all of their dinner . . .
(plus three pieces of cake, two chocolate bars, and sodas)."

✳ "They were as good as gold . . .
(until I told them to go to bed)."

✳ "There were no tantrums at all . . .
(mainly because I let them have their own way all night)."

✳ "They went to bed at seven-thirty on the dot . . .
(give or take an hour or two)."

✳ "They didn't watch any television . . .
(they just played computer games for three hours)."

✳ "The baby went to sleep right away . . .
(after three bottles of milk and two hours of screaming)."

✳ "I don't mind your being late . . .
(but I was ready for my bed three hours ago)."

✳ "I had a great evening — ask me anytime . . .
(just give me a month or two to recover first)."

*"If your baby is 'beautiful and perfect, never cries
or fusses, sleeps on schedule and burps on demand,
an angel all the time,' you're the grandma."*
TERESA BLOOMINGDALE, author

A Guide to Sleepovers

"Can you take the kids for the weekend?" There comes a time in all grandmas' lives when they hear these dreaded words and wonder if they are up to the task. Be flattered. No parents would leave their children behind unless they were certain they were in safe hands.

There are a few golden rules to stick to when the babysitting session turns into a weekend sleepover.

✳ If your house isn't already stocked with toys, tell the children to bring their own.

✳ If they have special bedtime toys, make sure they come, too. Bedtime without a favorite teddy bear won't be much fun!

✳ Buy a small gift, such as crayons and paper, paints, or crafts, and use it as a distraction for the moment the parents say good-bye.

✳ Don't tell very young children that Mommy and Daddy are going away. Instead say, "You're going to come stay with me so that we can have lots of fun."

✳ Turn the weekend into an adventure. Think of one or two activities in advance and tell them what they are so they will look forward to the weekend.

✳ Phone calls to and from parents should be limited to an emergency-only basis. Don't call Mom and Dad to find out where little Molly's toothbrush is or to tell them that Molly is refusing to go to bed. Advise Mom and Dad not to call as well. Children are capable of forgetting their parents for a few hours, but there's nothing like a call from Mommy to remind them that their parents are away. This can lead to many tears at bedtime. Out of sight is out of mind for most young children.

✳ Stick to the parental rules. The children might be on your territory now, but their parents won't thank you if the children come home spoiled rotten and refuse to go to bed because "Grandma let us stay up late."

✳ Don't feed the kids forbidden foods. You may not agree that the children should be denied lemonade and cookies, but it is not your decision to make. Give them treats, by all means, but nothing that would annoy their parents.

✳ Unless you already know your grandchildren inside out, get parents to write a list of likes and dislikes so that you're aware of any foods they simply won't eat.

✳ Don't worry if the angelic child you have looked after all weekend turns into a monster when Mom and Dad return. This is a natural reaction and is designed to punish the parents for their absence.

Household Essentials

If you're babysitting your grandchildren at your own home, there are a few things you should keep in the house at all times.

First-aid kit checklist (keep kit out of reach of children)

* Band-Aids (for young children, the ones with pictures on them often help to distract them when they're hurt)

* antiseptic cream, spray, or wipes (some sprays even have anesthetic qualities to dull the pain!)

* calamine lotion (for rashes and bug bites)

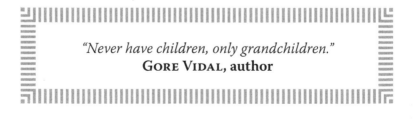

"Never have children, only grandchildren."
GORE VIDAL, author

* tweezers (for splinters, etc.)
* gauze, medical tape, and scissors

Useful foods to keep in stock

* bread
* cheese
* cans of tuna fish
* jam or jelly
* peanut butter (as long as your grandchildren have no nut allergies)
* milk
* yogurt
* chicken nuggets or fish fingers
* frozen peas
* eggs
* pasta
* spaghetti sauce
* hot chocolate/cocoa

Grandchildren essentials checklist

For the younger baby:

* changing mat

* diapers

* baby wipes

* diaper rash cream or ointment

* plastic bags (for dirty diapers)

* bottles

* formula (if bottle-fed)

For the older baby, add:

* unbreakable baby bowls

* spoons

* unbreakable drinking cups

* bibs

* baby food (even if you purée your own food, there are times when a jar is much more convenient)

For all ages:

* toys

* games

* books

* spare clothing (buy cheap T-shirts and pants and store them in a drawer for emergencies; keep hand-me-down rain boots for the next grandchild, etc.)

* sun hats and a winter hat

* sunscreen

In Grandma's Kitchen

One of the joys of having grandchildren around is teaching them how to cook. Moms and dads of very young children are often too busy feeding the family to show them how the food is prepared, but grandmas have had years of practice, and passing on your skills can be lots of fun.

Try to choose dishes that the kids will enjoy eating as well as cooking, and get them involved in making meals that they don't usually eat at home.

Baking cakes and muffins is ideal, as it means that they can take home the result of their hard work at the end of the day and share their goodies with Mom and Dad, too.

Working in the kitchen also teaches children about healthy eating habits.

A word of caution: Always remember that safety is very important and that young children should be kept away from hot pans, kettles, and ovens. It is also wise not to let the children "lick the bowl" if raw eggs have been used. Experts still advise against eating raw eggs, and many parents will not allow their children to lick a spoon or bowl with cake batter on it.

Here are a few ideas for some great things to make with the grandchildren.

Traditional Lemonade

MAKES EIGHT SERVINGS

When kids think of lemonade, they usually imagine the artificially sweetened store-bought variety, so this homemade version might take some getting used to. Remember to warn them that it will look cloudy. Homemade lemonade is a lovely, refreshing summer drink with no preservatives or artificial colors, but it does contain a lot of sugar. If you don't want it so sweet, try the low-sugar alternative.

Note that many young children and infants are allergic to citric acid, and it is not recommended to give citrus fruits to babies who are not yet a year old.

You will need:
6 lemons • 6 cups water
1 cup sugar • sprig of fresh mint (optional)

Method:

1 Using a potato peeler, peel the zest from two lemons and squeeze the juice from all six lemons.

2 Place the zest in a bowl, cover with the sugar, and pour over 1 cup of boiling water, then stir to make sure the sugar is properly dissolved. Allow to cool.

3 Strain this syrup into a serving pitcher, and stir in the juice and the remaining cold water.

4 Add mint, if desired, and serve chilled.

Make a special pink lemonade by adding a little cranberry juice. For a low-sugar alternative, skip the sugar syrup stage (step 2) and use 2 cups of white grape juice instead.

Chicken Nuggets

SERVES FOUR

Most kids love chicken nuggets, but the store-bought varieties aren't the most nutritious. These quick-and-easy nuggets will win the kids' approval, and you (and the children's parents) can rest assured that you know exactly what's in them.

You will need:
1 pound boneless, skinless chicken breasts
½ cup fresh bread crumbs
pinch of salt (optional)
1 egg
5 tablespoons sunflower or canola oil

Method:

1 Cut the chicken breasts into 2-inch-square chunks.

2 In a large bowl or shallow dish, mix the bread crumbs and salt (if using).

3 Beat the egg in a separate bowl.

4 Dip each chicken piece into the egg, then in the bread crumbs, turning until they are well coated.

⑤ Place the chicken pieces in bread crumbs on a baking sheet and chill in the fridge for 10 minutes.

⑥ Heat the oil in a large frying pan and fry the nuggets for 10 to 15 minutes, or until they are cooked through.

⑦ Remove excess oil by placing the nuggets on a paper towel, then serve with potato chips and ketchup.

Healthy Fruit Muffins

MAKES TWELVE

You will need:
¾ cup all-purpose flour
¾ cup whole wheat flour
1½ teaspoons baking powder
pinch of salt
¼ cup brown sugar
1 egg
3 tablespoons vegetable or canola oil
¾ cup milk
½ cup raisins or dried mixed fruit
12-cup muffin pan

Method:

① In a large bowl, mix together both types of flour, baking powder, salt, and the sugar.

② Add the egg and then slowly mix in the oil and the milk. Stir well.

③ Add the raisins or dried fruit and mix together.

④ Grease the muffin pan. Divide the mixture equally among the 12 cups in the pan.

⑤ Bake at 375°F for 15 to 20 minutes.

Chocolate Chip Cookies

MAKES APPROXIMATELY TWENTY

Making cookies is guaranteed to win over the grandchildren. Not only are they fun to bake, but they're also delicious to eat, and you can almost certainly make enough for them to take some home to Mom and Dad.

You will need:
4 tablespoons soft butter or margarine
½ cup soft light brown sugar
1 teaspoon pure vanilla extract
1 egg
½ cup all-purpose flour
½ cup chocolate chips

Method:

1. In a large bowl, beat the soft butter or margarine and sugar until pale and creamy.

2. Add the vanilla extract, egg, and flour. Beat together well.

3. Stir in the chocolate chips.

4. Grease two baking sheets.

5. Spoon dollops of the mixture onto the baking sheets, leaving space for the cookies to spread.

6. Bake the cookies at 350°F for about 8 minutes, or until golden.

7. Remove from the oven and leave to cool for about 10 minutes before transferring to a wire rack with a spatula.

Glamorous Grandmas

Sophia Loren

The sultry Italian star became a second-time grandmother in 2007, the same year that she appeared in a sexy Pirelli calendar at the age of seventy-two. The stunning septuagenarian is the oldest woman to appear in the famous calendar, and she looked fabulous.

"Of course, one wants to grow old gracefully," she said. "I like to take care of myself but I'm not afraid of getting wrinkles."

In fact, she uses the same products as her tiny grandson to keep her skin soft and youthful. "I like to use baby oil for cleansing my skin and baby shampoo to wash my hair, purely because they don't contain any harsh ingredients," she explained. "I never use any night cream on my face; just a little under-eye cream once I've removed my eye makeup."

Family is Sophia's passion and, as a relatively late mother to her sons, Carlo Ponti Jr. and Edoardo, she is thrilled to be a grandmother to Edoardo's daughter Lucia and Carlo's baby, Vittorio.

"He is the most beautiful baby in the world," she remarked when Vittorio was five weeks old. "He's wonderful and my son and his wife are so happy to have him. We just wait for him to say something and to do something for us. . . . If you blow on his face, he smiles."

Honor Blackman

Octogenarian Honor Blackman looks younger than most sixty-year-olds and has a more active life than people half her age.

The former Bond girl Pussy Galore and star of the British television series *The Avengers* shuns the idea of retirement and spent the year before her eightieth birthday on the grueling tour of her one-woman show.

Honor, who wrote a beauty book called *How to Look & Feel Half Your Age for the Rest of Your Life*, says keeping active and interested is the key to staying young.

"People ask me, 'Why do you last so well?' and I say, 'Because I've always got an interest in life,'" she revealed. "From the age of sixteen, I've always had something to do and somewhere to go."

The mother of two became a grandma at seventy-six and found herself with four grandchildren in three years. "I thought I'd have one foot in the grave before I had one, and all of a sudden it was like the number eleven bus and they all came along at once!" she said. "They're lovely."

Like many grandmas, Londoner Honor admits she would like her grandchildren to live nearer, since her daughter has moved to the country. "It's lovely for the kids," she explained. "But it's upsetting for poor old Grandmama."

"What's so simple even a small child can manipulate it? Why, a grandmother, of course!"
AUTHOR UNKNOWN

Joan Collins

Actress Joan Collins is the archetypal independent grand-mother. Although she adores her grandchildren, as soon as the first was born in 1998 she decided that she didn't want to be "Granny" or "Grandma." Instead, her grandchildren call her "DoDo."

Now in her seventies, the *Dynasty* star is married to hus-band number five, Percy Gibson, whom she met when she was sixty-eight and he was thirty-six.

"He loves my children and my baby grandchildren. So it works out really well," she said during a TV interview with Larry King. "We see the grandchildren quite often. And after a few weeks or a few days, we'd say, that's it, let's go back to having our own life and doing what we want to do and getting up when we want to, and not having to get up in the middle of the night."

Joan is famed for her youthful looks and says a healthy and balanced diet has kept her young. "I don't believe in eating junk and I protect my face all the time from the sun with base and makeup, even in the winter."

Although she clearly takes care of herself, she's characteris-tically dismissive of the idea of aging. "Age, in my opinion, has no bearing at all. That is, unless, of course, one happens to be a bottle of wine."

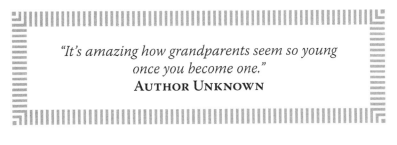

"It's amazing how grandparents seem so young once you become one."
AUTHOR UNKNOWN

Goldie Hawn

Blond, bubbly, and beautiful, it's hard to believe this movie star is a grandma, but in 2004, grandson Ryder was born to actress daughter Kate Hudson. However, Goldie immediately shunned traditional names for the apt moniker "Glamma."

The star of *The First Wives' Club* and *Private Benjamin* attributes her looks to her regular intake of "green fruit juice," along with the occasional carrot juice. Her miracle beverage apparently contains celery, parsley, kale, and peppers. Yum!

Grandma Goldie also sticks to a strict exercise regime. "I've never stopped working on my body," she has said. "I ride my bike up a mountain every day and I have to get on a running machine, do aerobics, or dance daily."

However, the Oscar-winning star also bemoaned the fate of aging female actresses in Hollywood when she said, "There are only three ages for women in Hollywood — Babe, District Attorney, and Driving Miss Daisy."

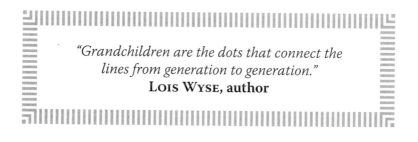

"Grandchildren are the dots that connect the lines from generation to generation."
LOIS WYSE, author

Games to Play with the Grandkids

Picture Consequences

At least three players
Ages three and up

You will need paper and pens or pencils.

1. Each player draws the head of an animal or person at the top of his or her piece of paper, making it as weird and funny as he or she likes. Then he or she folds the paper over until only the bottom of the head is visible.

2. The paper is handed to the left and the next player adds a neck to the drawing. That player then folds the paper down to cover the neck and passes it on to the person on the left.

3. This person draws a body of his or her choosing, folds the paper over as above, and leaves an indication of where the legs should join on.

4. The next player adds the legs and feet and folds the paper again, handing it to the left for the last time.

5. Each player opens up his or her piece of paper to reveal the bizarre artistic results.

Granny, May I?

Three or more players
Ages three and up

First, stand several steps away from the children with your back toward them. Then choose a child and give her an instruction, such as "Molly, you may take two giant steps toward me." Molly must then respond with "Granny, may I?" and you can say yes or no.

You can include different-size steps, such as giant, baby, or normal, and you can suggest silly styles like bunny hops and ballet steps. You can also make the children move backward.

If the child forgets to ask, "Granny, may I?," he or she must go back to the start. The object of the game is to be the first child to reach Granny, and so the winner is the first one to touch you.

Concentration (or Memory)

Two or more players
Ages four and up

You will need a standard fifty-two-card deck.

1. Shuffle the pack and spread the cards out in a pattern, facedown, on a table or floor.

2. Starting with the youngest child, each player turns over two cards. If a player gets a pair, he or she keeps the cards and takes another turn. If the cards do not match, all players try to remember what is on the cards, and the cards are turned facedown again.

③ The next player then turns over two cards and looks for a pair. Each pair found means the player gets another turn.

④ The game is over when all the cards have been picked up, and the winner is the player with the most pairs.

In the Manner of the Word

Two or more players
Ages eight and up

This game can be played anywhere and requires no equipment, but the more people involved, the better.

① One person is sent out of the room and the other players (or player) decide on an adverb that is easy to act out, such as *angrily* or *sadly*.

② The person outside the room is then called back in and asks the rest of the players to perform specific acts "in the manner of the word." For example, if the word is *angrily*, he or she could say to one player, "Pick up that book," and the player would pick up the book in an aggressive and angry manner. He or she could then ask the next player what the time is, which would also be done in an angry way.

③ The player continues to ask others to perform acts until he or she has guessed the word.

It is not necessary to score this game, but if you want to, you could award points for the number of "acts" requested before the correct guess, and the winner would be the person with the fewest points. You can also play this game in teams if there is a large number of people present.

Telegrams

Three or more players
Ages five and up

You will need pencils, paper, and a timer or watch with a second hand.

Each player picks a letter. All the letters are written in a column down the left-hand side of your paper. If there are only a few people playing, it may be necessary to go around two or three times, as you need a minimum of eight letters.

When all the letters are written down, players have two minutes to come up with a funny message in the style of a telegram, using the chosen letters to begin each word.

For example, if you had the letters M O W H S H T C, the telegram might read:

Mom's

On

Way

Home

Stop

Hide

The

Cat

Telegrams is not a competitive game, but it can still provide plenty of laughs. There's one thing to consider, though: In the era of e-mails and text messages, the old-fashioned concept of a telegram might need to be explained!

Growing Old Disgracefully

The traditional image of a grandma is a white-haired old lady who sits in her favorite chair knitting and telling stories of the good old days. But the twenty-first-century grandmother is a very different creature.

You are more likely to find her running around the yard playing football with her grandchildren than knitting bootees. Chances are Grandma has a career or has retired from one, and having been a busy mom herself, she is enjoying the time that she gets to spend with her grandchildren.

As a new millennium grandma, you're full of surprises! So the next time your children and grandchildren start to take you for granted, here are a few things you might want to do to make them stop and take notice:

* learn to fly a plane

* take up surfing (the waves rather than the Web)

* have some plastic surgery

* join a singles' club (but only if you are single!)

* dye your hair a shocking shade of pink

* go backpacking around the world
* buy a sports car

Things Modern-Day Grandmas Have Swapped . . .

* curlers for hair straighteners
* polyester for denim
* baking bread for being a breadwinner
* housework for house parties
* sewing for surfing the net
* needlepoint for Pilates
* sherry for Shiraz
* granny glasses for contact lenses

Hobbies to Impress the Grandchildren

* dance classes

* canoeing

* sailing

* acting in a local theater

* buying and selling on Internet auction sites

* guitar lessons

* carpentry

* making jewelry

* windsurfing

* playing computer games

* beekeeping

* rock climbing

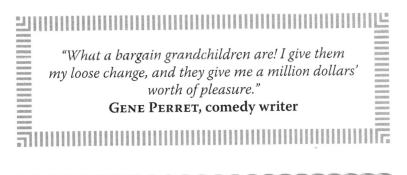

"What a bargain grandchildren are! I give them my loose change, and they give me a million dollars' worth of pleasure."
GENE PERRET, comedy writer

Don't Call Me Grandma!

You may be celebrating grandmotherhood, but that doesn't mean you feel old enough to be called Grandma or Granny. After all, the average age of a new grandparent is only forty-seven, so you're not ready for the crocheted shawl and rocking chair just yet.

An increasing number of new grandparents are shunning the traditional names, including celebrities such as Goldie Hawn, who opted to be called Glamma. Being called by your first name is not advisable, however, as it can send confusing messages to the children and can make them unsure of your relationship to them.

Some favorite alternatives include Nanna, Nanny, Grammy, Gammy, and Grams. But if you prefer something a little bit different, why not try some foreign-language options:

* Babka — Polish

* Lola — Filipino

* Mémé — French

* Mummo — Finnish

* Nonna — Italian

* Oma — German

* Sobo — Japanese

* Ugogo — Zulu

Or how about "Moogie," which is used in sci-fi TV shows *Star Trek* and *Deep Space Nine*?

Perfect Present Buying

The art of buying the perfect gift for your grandchild is a fine balancing act. Always remember that, as well as pleasing the recipient of the gift, you must avoid annoying the parents, who will have to live with the consequences of your choice.

Before picking up the biggest plastic electronic toy in the store, imagine a scene in your son's or daughter's house, after the toy has been opened. Then ask yourself the following important questions:

✳ Do they have the space for it?

✳ Where will they put it?

✳ Is it easy to assemble/dismantle?

✳ Does it go back in the box?

✳ Does your grandchild have a million similar toys?

✳ Is it too noisy?

As a rule, parents tend to like presents that are educational, fun, reasonably small, and that won't be discarded or fall apart within days.

Best Baby Presents

When there is a bundle of joy on the way, the world seems to be full of the cutest cuddly toys. As a grandparent, though, it pays to think practically. Ask your children what they would like you to buy and tell them how much you want to spend.

That way they'll know whether you're willing to splurge on a car seat or if you just want to buy some clothes. Here are some suggestions that should win the vote of parents-to-be.

Baby basket

Fill a huge basket with diapers, wipes, and a baby-size robe, as well as baby bubble bath and soap, and a few beauty treats for the new mom. Not only will it be appreciated, but it will save the parents a lot of money.

Bedding

A pretty blanket or quilt is always useful. You could also throw in a few sheets for the crib, too.

Activity center for the crib

These are great for stimulating babies when they are old enough to push buttons and ring bells.

Baby gym

The baby lies on a mat underneath two arches with toys suspended from them. It'll keep him or her amused for hours.

Lullaby night-light

There are some great nursery lights on the market that project interesting shapes on the walls and ceiling.

Interactive plush toy

If you do want to buy something cute and cuddly, make it an electronic toy that teaches baby to press buttons to hear music and nursery rhymes.

Door bouncer

These hold babies safely while they gently bounce. Babies love them! In order to use a door bouncer, a baby must be able to hold his or her head up unassisted. Always follow the manufacturer's installation and safety instructions, and never leave a baby in a door bouncer unsupervised.

Children's savings bonds/account

Grandmothers can build up a nest-egg for their grandchildren by buying bonds or opening a savings account in their names, and putting in money on birthdays or at Christmas. The kids will be thrilled when they're old enough to make use of Grandma's generous gift.

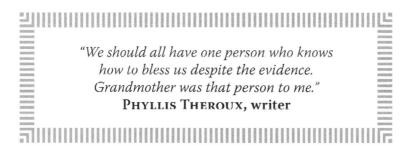

"We should all have one person who knows how to bless us despite the evidence. Grandmother was that person to me."
PHYLLIS THEROUX, writer

Worst Baby Presents

Plush toys

As a grandmother it is your duty NEVER to add to the plush toy mountain that inevitably accumulates in every small child's bedroom!

Newborn baby clothes

If you do want to buy baby clothes, never buy newborn size. Lots of other people will, so be practical. In six to nine months, no one will be buying gifts, so choose outfits for then, but make sure you take the season into account. It's no good buying a winter coat for a six- to nine-month-old if your grandchild is born in December!

Designer clothes

There really is no point in buying Dolce & Gabbana shirts for a person who is going to dribble sour milk and orange baby food down them all day.

Shoes

There are expensive shoes and sneakers on the market for babies, but until children are at least six months old, these shoes are pretty pointless and also not good for a child's feet. Inexpensive fabric bootees (or knitted ones if you are a really traditional grandma) will keep babies' feet warm. Let's face it, your grandchild isn't going to be running a marathon anytime soon.

Best Presents for Older Children

Wooden fort or dollhouse

As long as your son or daughter has room indoors, forts and dollhouses are still wonderful toys. This gift also solves present-buying quandaries for the future, as there will always be a list of new items to add.

White board

A drawing board complete with wipe-clean marker pens makes a wonderful gift and will save on the mound of paper and endless paintings that moms feel obligated not to throw away.

Computer game

Most families have a computer, and there are hundreds of games available that are educational as well as fun.

Building toys

LEGO and its equivalents are still very popular with kids, and their versatility means a child will never get bored.

Sports equipment

If the children have a backyard, new athletic gear encourages them to be active. Golf sets and badminton sets are widely available in children's sizes, and you can't go wrong with a soccer ball, whatever age and sex the kids are.

Watch

For a child over the age of five, a watch is a great gift, as it will encourage your grandchild to tell the time.

Art set

Markers, pencils, and paints are always running out, so big sets of art materials make perfect, creative gifts.

Bike

If you can afford it, a bicycle is most likely to be welcomed by both adult and child. Who doesn't like the idea of a new bike?

Books

You can never have too many.

Electronic reading system

Perfect for preschool learning, although electronic reading systems aren't cheap.

Worst Presents for Older Children

Crying baby doll

Unless it comes with an off switch and your grandchild plays with it only in her bedroom, a crying baby doll is a gift parents despise.

High-maintenance toys

It's a nice gesture buying your little darlings the latest remote-control car or robotic dinosaur, but if the remote requires four batteries and the toy requires another six, think again. You might provide the batteries the first time, but three days later when they run out, it will be up to the parents to keep replacing them.

Drum kit

Avoid drums of any kind.

Guns

Boys may gravitate on their own toward playing with guns, but these days many parents shy away from providing them. If so, these parents won't thank you for buying their son a plastic semiautomatic so he can pretend to murder his sister!

A puppy or another pet

Don't ever give an animal as a gift unless you have the approval of the parents first!

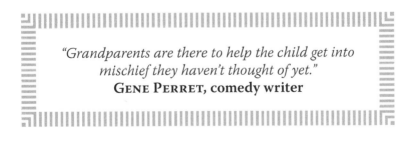

"Grandparents are there to help the child get into mischief they haven't thought of yet."
GENE PERRET, comedy writer

Grandma's Lotions and Potions

Traditional remedies are passed down from generation to generation, but how many of them really work? Here are the scientific explanations behind some of the most effective age-old cures for everyday ailments.

Wasp and bee stings

First and most important, if your grandchild shows any signs of an allergic reaction after a wasp or bee sting, seek medical attention immediately. If there's no sign of an allergy, try a home remedy to soothe the sting. For a bee sting, always remove the stinger as quickly as possible. It's okay to pull it out with your fingers. Bees and ants have acidic stings, which means an alkali is needed to neutralize the acid. For this

reason the best treatment for a bee sting is baking soda or even unperfumed soap. Conversely, the wasp's sting is alkaline, so the best thing for it is an acid such as vinegar.

If you find it difficult to remember which sting needs which treatment, just tell yourself "Bee" for baking soda.

Toothache

Chewing cloves or using clove oil has long been regarded as a great cure for a toothache. The reason it works is the large concentration of a substance called eugenol, which has anti-microbial properties that restrict the growth of bacteria and viruses. It is also a mild anesthetic and anti-inflammatory, which helps to relieve the pain.

To cure a bout of toothache, one or two cloves can be chewed, or an oil of cloves product can be rubbed on the gums. Be aware, though, that full-strength oil of cloves should not be used, as it can damage nerves. It's best to check with a pharmacist before buying a product containing oil of cloves.

Fresh figs also contain an anti-inflammatory agent, and when rubbed on the gums they are a good alternative cure for young children if clove products are too bitter.

If the toothache persists, take your grandchild to a dentist.

Hay fever

Some say unfiltered honey from local bees is a natural preventative to the yearly onslaught of hay fever. Sufferers can take one spoonful of locally produced honey every day, all year round. This may deliver a tiny daily dose of pollen from that area. This way the body may build a resistance to the pollen that triggers an attack, so that when spring arrives the body won't react so violently.

A word of caution: Never give honey or corn syrup to babies who are less than a year old, as the spores in honey can cause infant botulism.

Cuts

You may have heard of rubbing salt in wounds (not recommended, obviously), but what about pepper? Black pepper placed directly on a cleaned external cut will stop the bleeding and, amazingly, it doesn't sting. Cayenne pepper is also effective. If the cut is deep, medical help should always be sought, but the pepper will stem the bleeding in the meantime, especially if you pack the wound.

Cayenne pepper can also be used to stop nosebleeds, and a poultice of the pepper wrapped around a wound is also thought to reduce scarring.

Earwax

A child's ear is a delicate instrument, and a buildup of wax might make them want to dig their fingers inside, thereby causing damage. Olive oil is a simple, cheap, and effective way of softening and clearing wax. Warm some olive oil to body temperature and then, using a ear dropper, put one or two drops into the ear. Repeat once or twice a day until the wax clears. If the wax doesn't clear and is impacted, see a doctor to have it removed.

A word of caution: If the child is suffering any discomfort, pain, or fever, do not put in drops. Instead, see a doctor immediately.

Olive oil is also a perfect remedy for dry skin in babies. Rather than using manufactured baby oil, rub a few drops of olive oil between your palms and then smooth it over baby's skin.

Colds and sinusitis

If your grandchild's nose is congested, a homemade lemonade will give him or her a lift. Dissolve a teaspoon of honey in a mug of hot water and add it to the juice of four lemons and one orange (optional). Then add 4 cups of cold water and refrigerate.

The drink will help ease congestion by cutting mucus production. It also provides a boost of vitamin C, which helps fight a cold. This is a child-friendly, nonalcoholic version of the traditional hot toddy.

Insomnia

Every grandma knows that lavender is a natural promoter of sleep. If your grandchildren are staying over while Mom and Dad are out enjoying themselves, a drop of lavender oil on a pillow or in the bedtime bath might help them to fall asleep, provided a child doesn't have an allergy to lavender.

It Never Did Us Any Harm . . .

If you were brought up on a daily dose of cod liver oil, you might want to know if it did you more harm than good. Were your parents misled, or could the youth of today still benefit from the odd dose of a foul-tasting formula?

Cod liver oil

The long-held belief that fish oil is good for growing brains seems to have been proven true by recent research. Fish oils contain omega-3 fatty acids, which are important for nerve function. Children with low omega-3 levels in their bodies have been found to be more likely to be hyperactive and display behavior problems. Some studies have shown that supplements can help children with dyslexia and attention deficit disorders.

Omega-3s can be found in a natural diet, of course, with oily fish such as sardines, mackerel, and salmon as the best providers. Given that fish is not the favorite food of most kids, however, a supplement might be an idea. These days, health food stores carry specially designed formulas for kids that actually taste good.

Castor oil

Grandmas throughout the centuries have used a dose of castor oil to flush out the system, and it certainly does have purgative properties. However, its laxative powers are so strong it is no longer recommended for children under twelve or for prolonged use.

Syrup of figs

Figs are known for their mild laxative properties, and the syrup made from the fruit is a traditional cure for constipation. Originating from natural products, the liquid is suitable for children and is still available, and effective, today. The taste is an acquired one, though, so getting a fussy child to swallow a dose isn't always easy.

Chicken soup

The loveliest and most soothing of remedies for a child with a cold is Grandma's homemade chicken soup. The soup helps to boost the immune system, slows down the production of mucus, and provides much-needed nutrition. So get cooking!

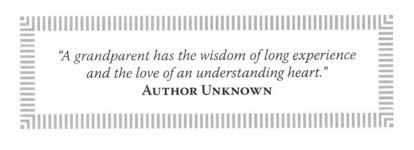

"A grandparent has the wisdom of long experience and the love of an understanding heart."
AUTHOR UNKNOWN

Grandma's Arts and Crafts

A Card for All Occasions

Discount stores, certain supermarkets, and stationery and craft stores sell packs of colored card stock and paper, so it is worth investing in a few of these if you have grandchildren. As you will remember from your own kids, a homemade Mother's Day card is the best kind.

Colored paper always looks pretty, but make sure it's not too dark as it will be more difficult to write and draw on. Remember to handle the scissors yourself when you're working with very young children.

Patchwork heart

This is a great card design because it requires little artistic skill and even very young children can help.

You will need:
a thin piece of card stock
colored pens or pencils
scissors
scraps of wrapping paper, magazine pages,
foil, and/or crepe paper
craft glue
glitter (optional)

1 Start by folding the two shorter edges of the card stock together to create a greeting-card shape.

2 On the front of the card, draw a large heart. Make sure

it's in the center and leave space at the top for the word "MOM," which should be in big letters.

3 Cut up scraps of wrapping paper, foil, crepe paper, and magazine pages featuring attractive designs. Make sure that the scissors are not too sharp if your grandchild is doing the cutting, and keep a close eye on him or her at all times.

4 Cover the heart with glue and get your grandchild to stick the paper scraps within the heart, making sure that they don't go over the edge and distort the shape.

5 At the top of the page write "MOM" in block letters and fill in with glue.

6 Over a newspaper, sprinkle glitter over the top of the card and then shake off the excess, leaving behind a sparkling "MOM."

7 Write your message inside.

A word of caution: Not all moms will appreciate a card that spreads glitter all over the house, so the word "MOM" could be colored in with paints or pens instead. However, if you feel like wreaking revenge for all the time you spent vacuuming glitter from the furniture when your own kids were young, sprinkle away!

Crêpe-paper creation

Using pieces of different-colored crepe paper, you and your grandchild can make a beautifully decorated card suitable for any occasion.

1. Fold the card as in the previous step 1 and get your grandchild to draw a picture on the front. It could be a scene of the whole family, of Mom, or of a bunch of flowers.

2. Put blobs of glue in the places where you want to stick the crepe paper. For example, the clothes of family figures, the petals of flowers, or individual flowers in a garden can all be created with crepe paper.

3. Crumple up the scraps of different-colored crepe paper into tiny balls and stick them onto the glue.

4. When the glue has dried, color in the remaining picture and write your message.

✳ ✳ ✳

Father's Day shirt-and-tie card

This is a really effective and simple card for Father's Day, and the message can be hidden under the tie.

You will need:
scissors
1 sheet of heavy card stock or a cereal box
ruler
2 sheets of white 8½ x 11 paper
glue
construction paper or thick card stock for the tie
colored markers or crayons

1. Cut the piece of card stock (or one side of the cereal box) so that it measures 5 inches by 8 inches.

2. Take a sheet of white paper and place it down horizontally. Then place the card stock in the center of the white paper vertically.

3. Fold the white paper over the card stock so that it covers it completely, and glue it down on the back.

4. To create a collar effect on the shirt, cut the top of the card stock into an "M" shape, then fold down the two peaks.

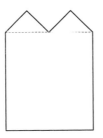

5. Next, using the construction paper or thick card stock, cut out a tie shape.

6. Use markers or crayons to design a funky pattern on the tie.

7 Glue the top of the tie to the card stock, ensuring that the rest of the tie can move up and down freely.

8 Glue the collar flaps down onto the shirt.

9 Write a message on the underside of the tie, such as "Happy Father's Day!" or "To the World's Best Dad!"

10 Now lift the tie and draw a straight line down the middle of the front of the shirt. You can then draw on some buttons and color them in.

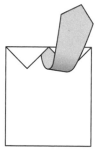

11 You could also draw a pocket on either side of the tie.

12 To make the card stand up by itself, cut another piece of card stock into a rectangle measuring 5 inches by 2 inches. Measure ¾ inch from the edge, fold the card stock over, and glue the bent part onto the back of your card to help to keep it upright.

Pop-up Easter card

Perfect for Easter, this clever card is easy to make, lots of fun, and is certain to keep the grandkids amused, especially younger ones.

You will need:
2 pieces of very thick paper in different colors
scissors
glue
colored markers, pencils, or crayons

1. Fold one piece of paper in half, then, midway down the paper, cut a line of about 2 inches from the left-hand crease.

2. Fold back each of the flaps to make two triangles, thereby making a large triangular hole at the spine.

3. Run your fingernail along the triangle edges to make sure the creases are sharp.

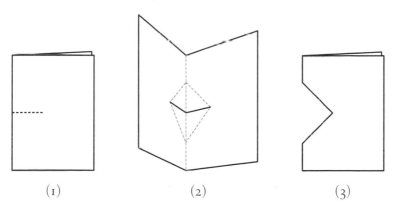

(1)   (2)   (3)

4. Straighten the triangles and open the card about halfway (resting it on your knees is a good way to keep it from lying flat).

⑤ Push one of the triangles through the hole and pinch to make it stand up. Repeat with the other triangle.

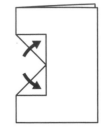

⑥ Close the card and push down on the folds to make them well creased. When it is opened, you should now have a pop-up beak.

⑦ Fold the second piece of paper in half, glue around the inside edges, and stick to the back of the pop-up card, making sure the glue does not go near the beak.

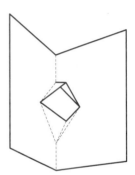

⑧ Finally, you can have some fun drawing a bird's face around the beak and decorating the front of your card as you wish. You might want to add an Easter message and some spring flowers.

3-D Christmas tree card

What better way to prepare for Christmas than to help the grandkids create a unique 3-D tree card, adorned with colorful decorations?

You will need:
1 sheet white card stock
colored pens or pencils
ruler
scissors
2 sheets green card stock
1 sheet brown card stock
1 sheet red card stock
glue
paint, beads, silver foil, gold and silver
star stickers, glitter, sequins, etc.

1. Using the white card stock, make a template by cutting a rectangle measuring 5 inches by 8 inches. Fold it in half vertically so it is 2½ inches wide.

2. Draw three horizontal lines to divide the card into four equal sections, each with a height of 2 inches.

3. The top three sections will form the main part of the tree. Draw a steep diagonal line from the top of the crease to a third of the way across the first line. Then draw two more

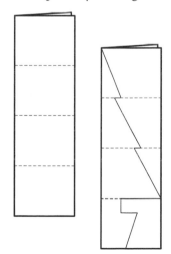

staggered diagonal lines underneath to form the basic shape (see diagram on page 63).

④ Next, draw the trunk and a container shape in the bottom section.

⑤ Carefully cut out the shape across the fold and open it up.

⑥ Place this template over both sheets of the green card stock and cut out two identical shapes.

⑦ Decorate the green trees by gluing on your silver foil, sequins, beads, and paint. Add some glitter if you like. Cover the trunk with a small piece of brown card stock and the container with some of the red card stock.

⑧ When the decorations have dried, cut a 4-inch slit down the center of one of the trees from the top. Then, cut another 4-inch slit up from the bottom of the other tree.

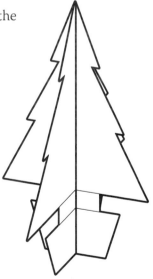

⑨ Slide the two trees together to form a cross at the base.

⑩ Add a gold or silver foil star sticker at the top to hold everything in place.

You can put the finishing touches on your pretty 3-D Christmas tree by writing a message on the container.

Celebrities and Their Grandmothers

50 Cent's soft side

Rapper 50 Cent may have a tough-guy image, but he's devoted to his grandma! Born Curtis James Jackson III, "50" was taken in by his grandma after his mother died when he was only eight. However, despite her best efforts, his grandmother couldn't keep young Curtis on the straight and narrow, and he took up drug dealing and ran with gangs from an early age. He later reflected, "I became two people — one was the hard-core drug dealer in the day, and the other was my grandmother's baby by night."

When his gangster lifestyle caught up with him, the young rapper was shot nine times outside his grandmother's house, while his own baby son slept inside. With stints in jail and a troubled past behind him, 50 Cent is now one of the best-selling rap artists in the world, and still remains very close to his grandma.

He used some of his newfound riches to buy her a new house and, when he was lacking inspiration for his album *Curtis*, he returned to her old home, a cramped basement in Queens, New York.

"I wrote and recorded lyrics for this album at my grandmother's house again," he said on the album's release. "I went back in the basement, where you have to bend down the ceiling is so low, where I wrote [hit album] *Get Rich or Die Tryin'*. Being in that environment helped me remember things. . . ."

Style guru

Actress Rosario Dawson thinks her grandmother is so cool that she swaps clothes with her! The beautiful star of *Sin City* regularly raids her grandmother's closet and shares an occasional beer with her, too.

"My grandmother just turned seventy-one," she explained in 2006. "We drink Bud and hang out. Normally I wear her clothes. We're the exact same size, so it works out really well.

"She's from Puerto Rico and her English is still not 100 percent. She'll be like, 'Rosario, look at the alligator on the window,' and it's actually a lizard. Or she'll say, 'Look at the carpenter bird,' and it will be a woodpecker. Just like really, really cute stuff. It's adorable. I love her!"

Message from beyond

Actress Jennifer Love Hewitt believes she was contacted by her dead grandmother while she was making a television show. The star of *I Know What You Did Last Summer* was filming an episode of *Ghost Whisperer* at the time. In the show, which was developed by spiritual medium James Van Praagh, Jennifer plays the part of Melinda Gordon, a young woman who can see and communicate with the dead.

One night, during a session directed by Van Praagh, Hewitt says her dead grandmother made herself known. "We had an evening with James where he did this thing and my grandmother came through," she revealed. "She just wanted to say hello and tell me that she was looking out for me. It was really nice."

Where there's a Will . . .

Before marrying Jada Pinkett-Smith, funny guy Will Smith took her to meet his grandmother, but things didn't go well.

"When I met Will's grandmother it was pretty embarrassing," a cringing Jada once recalled. "I walked in and she had just finished watching *Jason's Lyric*. I have a pretty explicit love scene in that movie. I walked in and Will says, 'This is Jada.'

"She kind of looked at me and said, 'I just don't know why young people feel like they gotta take their clothes off all the time.' I looked at Will like, 'Is this a joke?' I can look at it now and think it's pretty funny, but [at the time] I was really upset."

Guess who had recommended the film to dear old Grandma — Will, of course!

Granny's shame

Eva Longoria was delighted to win the role of sexy Gabrielle Solis in *Desperate Housewives*, but her grandmother was less than impressed. In fact, she even stopped talking to the actress altogether.

"She is an old, traditional Mexican grandma," explained the actress. "She doesn't really get the whole acting thing. She doesn't understand the profession of acting. She was like,

'What were you doing on TV with that boy!' I was like, 'Grandma, it's fake; it's not real.'

"I tried to think of every adjective I could think of. So I said, 'It's a lie.' And she said, 'Why are you lying! That's worse!'"

Diddy little twins

Hip-hop celebrity Diddy honored two precious grandmothers when he and girlfriend Kim Porter had their twin girls in December 2006. The babies were named Jessie James and D'Lila Star after the star's grandma Jessie Smalls and Kim's grandmother Lila Star.

"In honor of the two people to have incredibly impacted me and Kim, we're proud to announce that we are naming the twins after our beloved grandmothers," the singer once said.

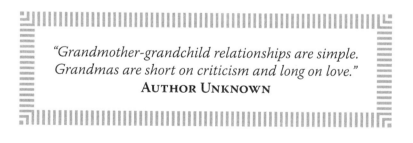

"Grandmother-grandchild relationships are simple. Grandmas are short on criticism and long on love."
AUTHOR UNKNOWN

Grandma Green Thumb

Gardening is a wonderful thing to do with your grandchildren, and it can be both fun and educational for them, too.

If you have room, set aside a little part of a flower bed for them to grow plants that they've chosen themselves. If space is limited, help them to plant a container or window box with their favorite flowers.

Start them off young; garden centers and toy stores often sell gardening kits for tiny hands. Invest in a mini watering can so that even a toddler can join in the fun, watering your garden or containers for you as a play activity.

Plants

The plants you choose will depend on many factors. Take into consideration the space you have, climate conditions, and whether the site is sunny, shady, or partly in the shade.

If your grandchildren are regular visitors, they will be able to take care of their plants and will be excited to see the progress of their own little patch every time they come. If visits are rare, try to choose plants that will last throughout the year, such as rosebushes or shrubs, rather than those that flower briefly, such as daffodils. That way the grandchildren won't be disappointed to find they have missed seeing their flowers in full bloom.

Dangerous plants

Always be sure the plants you choose to grow are not poisonous to young children. Make sure that you teach the children *never* to put anything from the garden in their mouth without asking a grown-up first.

This is a list of some of the most common plants for children to avoid in the garden, but always check when buying any new plants that they are safe for young children.

Bleeding heart	Larkspur
Daphne	Lily of the valley
Foxglove	Oleander
Fuchsia	Poppy
Holly	Rhubarb
Ivy	Wisteria

Summer Color

Here are a few suggestions for plants that are perfect for introducing a child to the delights of gardening. Of course there are many more on the market, and you may have your own favorites to share with your grandchildren.

For shady areas

Fuchsias and astilbes are ideal for containers and beds in a shady area and are very colorful when they flower. Fuchsias bloom between August and October, and astilbes blossom from June to August. Begonias make a colorful splash in the summer, too, but be sure to select the right variety, as many are houseplants. Cyclamens also provide nice ground cover and color.

For greenery, ferns and hostas are best for shady spots.

For sunny areas

The choice of flowers for sunny areas is endless, but children's favorites include pansies, sweet peas, lilies, and daisies. Roses are also very popular, and come in a huge range of colors and varieties. Patio roses are wonderful if you want to plant in containers, and a small rosebush really brightens up a flower bed. If you have a blank wall, a climbing rose in a pot or a flower bed is a nice option. Sunflowers are fabulous to grow in a sheltered sunny spot, and kids love to see how tall their bloom will grow.

If you're looking for green plants, herbs are the perfect plant to grow in the sun. Try thyme, basil, parsley, or mint. Not only are they decorative, but they can be useful when cooking, too.

Spring's Eternal

Create a container or a small flower bed that will produce new flowers throughout the spring. Planting bulbs is one of the easiest ways for children to start gardening and, if you plant in the autumn, you can produce a spectacular spring display.

Daffodils, tulips, and crocuses are all great plants to start with. However, all of these bulbs are poisonous if eaten, so make sure that young children are watched at all times while planting and that they wash their hands thoroughly after handling them.

Choose flower varieties that will blossom in early spring (crocuses and daffodils), mid-spring (hyacinths), and late spring (tulips). Plant them in good soil and compost, and wait for the fantastic results.

Hanging Baskets

Any outdoor area can be brightened up with spring and summer baskets. They are readily available online or in garden stores, as well as some supermarkets and home improvement stores.

If the basket you buy is unlined, you will need to line it with some plastic sheeting. You can put moss underneath the sheeting to improve the look of the bottom of the basket.

If using plastic, make sure you cut three slits in the lining (measuring about 1 inch) to allow excess water to escape. Plan how you're going to arrange your basket first, putting taller plants in the center and trailing plants on the outside. Ideal plants for hanging baskets are trailing fuchsias, impatiens, trailing geraniums, and lobelias. For the top, bush geraniums, petunias, and fuchsias are among the best, although there are plenty of other varieties that will work as well.

When you've lined your basket, fill it halfway with a soil-based compost. Add the side plants (lobelias, trailing geraniums, etc.) by making a small hole in the liner or moss and inserting the plant, root first, through it, making sure that the roots reach the compost.

The next step is to fill the basket with compost to about one inch from the top, leaving a slight slope down toward the center, then plant your other varieties. Start at the center and work your way out. Fill any gaps with border plants such as lobelias and petunias, and use trailing varieties for the edges.

The basket can be planted in early spring, but do not put it outside until the last frost has gone. Water the basket daily.

If you have nowhere to hang a basket, wall planters (containers that are nailed or screwed to the wall) are an inexpensive and pretty alternative.

Growing Vegetables

You don't have to have a huge garden to grow your own produce. Windowsill gardens and window boxes are both space-saving alternatives you can use to grow your own organic fruits and vegetables, and the children will be excited to try something healthy if they helped grow it.

For your vegetable garden, choose a food that you will enjoy eating fresh and that you will want to eat often. Salad greens are a good choice, and there are hundreds of varieties available as seeds. For variety, though, you could also buy a pack of mixed salad seeds.

Pepper, eggplant, and tomato leaves and stems are poisonous to young children, so although they are easy to grow, it's best to avoid those vegetables if you are likely to have toddlers wandering around. Other plants that do well in backyard gardens are zucchini, string beans, and corn.

If you don't think you have a green thumb, and you've never grown your own food before, don't worry. It isn't very hard. And just imagine the thrill of biting into a juicy corn on the cob with your grandchild, having picked it from your own garden!

Grandma's House of Fun

Making the children's visit to your house fun is what being a twenty-first-century grandma is all about. Long gone are the days when children visiting their grandparents were expected to be seen and not heard, speak when they were spoken to, and were forced to sit on the sofa listening to grown-up talk all day.

These days, one in two people age fifty-four is a grandparent, so grandmothers are often younger and fitter than in years gone by. And with more moms returning to work, grandmothers are also much more likely to be playing a major role in general child care.

With Mom and Dad often too busy to spend a great deal of time playing with the kids, the most important things you can give your grandchildren are time and attention. They are valuable commodities, and the children are guaranteed to look forward to the next time Grandma is in charge!

Things to Keep at Home

The amount of paraphernalia you keep at home for your grandchildren will, of course, be dictated by storage space, but here are a few suggestions.

Assorted jigsaw puzzles and board games

To save money, look for games and puzzles at garage sales and in secondhand stores.

Dress-up box

Instead of throwing out old clothes, hats, shoes, and bags, keep them all in a trunk or an old suitcase and have dressing-up days.

Paper, pens, and paints

Stacks of old paper mean hours of fun with the kids, and if you have a place where they can be messy with paints, that's even better, especially if Mom prefers not to have painting sessions at home. A word of warning, though — try not to send them home with their best outfit covered in paint!

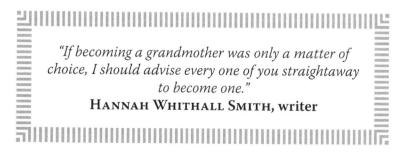

"If becoming a grandmother was only a matter of choice, I should advise every one of you straightaway to become one."
HANNAH WHITHALL SMITH, writer

Collage materials

Old scraps of ribbon, wrapping paper, foil, and sequins are perfect for a crafty afternoon. Also, building up collections of buttons, feathers, beads, and fabric will prove useful in the long term.

Outdoor games

Always keep a ball or two in the garage. A soccer ball is essential, even if you don't have a backyard, as you can always take it to the park. If space is limited, an inflatable beach ball is a good idea. If you have plenty of storage, you might like to pick up some inexpensive tennis rackets if there are courts nearby.

Inflatable pool

For hot days, nothing is more fun than splashing around in an inflatable pool. But be extra careful if you have young grandchildren, and *never* leave them unattended near the water.

Things to Do at Home

Make your own play dough

Store-bought play dough is expensive and often dries up very quickly. Making it yourself (with your grandchildren's help, of course!) can be a fun way to spend an afternoon.

You will need:
2 cups all-purpose flour
1 cup salt
¼ cup cream of tartar

2 cups water
2 tablespoons vegetable or sunflower oil
food coloring

1. Mix the flour, salt, and cream of tartar in a saucepan.

2. Add the water, oil, and food coloring and stir until smooth.

3. Cook over low heat for 4 to 5 minutes, stirring constantly. The dough should thicken into a mashed potato consistency. Set aside to cool.

As soon as you can handle the dough, you can get creative with it, but make sure you store it in an airtight container when you've finished playing so that it keeps for a few months.

A word of caution: Although the dough is made from edible ingredients, it should not be eaten, as its high salt content could harm a child.

Scavenger hunt

Your grandchildren will love a scavenger hunt, whether it is in the backyard or in the house, and organizing one requires minimum effort from you!

All you need to do is to write out a list of items, which will depend on the environment in which the hunt will take place. In the house, for example, your list could include a pencil, a spoon, a comb, and an object with flowers on it. In the backyard, you could request a fallen leaf, a ball, a stick, and an acorn. The list can be as short or long as you like.

Give the list to each child, along with a bag for collecting the objects, and send him or her out to look. The first child to come back to you with all the correct items is the winner. Have a small prize available for the winner.

Yarn hunt

This activity works best with a lot of children.

Take several different-colored balls of yarn and cut as many short pieces from each ball as there are children. Then hide the strands of yarn around the house in bunches of the same color, and tell the children how many colors they have to find.

The first child to return to you with strands of every color is the winner!

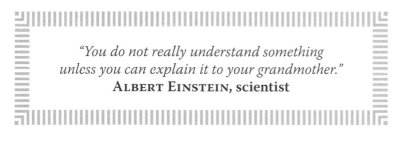

"You do not really understand something unless you can explain it to your grandmother."
ALBERT EINSTEIN, scientist

Craft kits

Most toy stores and supermarkets have an inexpensive range of craft kits that are great to stock up on. Children can create their own jewelry, handbags, dinosaurs, piggy banks, and model airplanes.

If you want to buy these kits as a gift, suggest keeping them at your house. You are much more likely to have the time to sit down with your grandkids and help them with the activities than their parents will be!

Dinosaur dig

This fun game is ideal if you have a sandbox in your backyard.

First, buy a dinosaur model kit with lots of parts (available at most toy stores). Number each separate part with a marker, so that you will know when each piece has been found, then bury the dino bones in a large quantity of sand.

Give the children a new two-inch paintbrush each, to give an authentic archaeological feel to the dig, and send them out to forage for the bones.

When the bones are all dug up, help the kids to build the dinosaur. It's a perfect way to spend an afternoon at Grandma's!

Crafty Advice

* Before you do anything, make sure you set up art projects in places where messy spills are easy to clean up, and always put down a mat or old newspapers before you start.

* Keep an old jelly jar as a water pot for painting, otherwise you might end up with paint stains all over your best china teacups!

* Even "washable" paint doesn't always come out of clothes. Keep a few old T-shirts to slip over the children's clothes to avoid getting in trouble with Mom and Dad.

* When your grandchild has put the finishing touches to his or her painting, if the subject of the masterpiece isn't immediately apparent, don't ask, "What is it?" Instead say, "Tell me about your picture."

* Keep a special place to exhibit their works of art. It doesn't have to be on your living room wall — a fridge or a wall in the den or home office is ideal.

* Buy a scrapbook. It's a really nice way of

keeping the occasional painting, card, and letter from your grandchildren.

✳ Don't try to keep everything your grandchild creates — you'll disappear under a mountain of paper in no time!

Potato printing

You may remember doing this with your own children or even when you were a child yourself, so why not repeat the experience with your grandchildren?

You will need:
sharp knife
several large potatoes
paper or cardboard
pencil
scissors
poster paint
paper plates

1 Cut your potatoes crosswise in half (make sure *you* do this and not your grandkids, as you don't want any accidents).

2 Get your grandchild to draw a small simple shape on a piece of paper. A star, a moon, a fish, or a smiley face are all good things to start with.

3 Cut out the shape with the scissors and trace it onto the cut surface of the potato.

4 Then, using the knife, carefully carve the background away, ¼- to ½-inch deep, leaving the shape intact. (Again, *you* must do this part.)

5 Pour thin layers of the paint onto the paper plates.

6. Dip the carved potato into the paint and firmly press the potato onto a piece of paper to create a clear impression of the shape.

7. When your grandkids have had enough of one shape, use the other half of the potato and make a new shape.

Pasta picture

Kids love making these simple pictures, and you can probably find the supplies in your pantry. Make sure you put a mat or newspaper on your table first, though, as this activity can get messy!

You will need:
pasta of various shapes, sizes, and colors
(penne, farfalle, macaroni, fusilli, etc.)
resealable plastic freezer bags
food coloring
newspaper
rice
empty plastic containers
paper
craft glue

1. If your pasta is not colored, place a handful of pasta shapes into a freezer bag and add a few drops of food coloring.

2. Shake well and then place the pasta onto newspaper to dry.

3. Repeat with as many different pastas and colors as you wish.

4. Place the rice into a few separate containers (such as empty plastic yogurt containers) and mix a drop or two of

food coloring in each. Add more drops if you want a stronger shade. Shake well and then leave to dry.

⑤ Put all the dried pasta shapes and rice into separate containers in the middle of the table or activity area (on newspaper, of course).

⑥ The children can either draw a picture and then glue on the pasta and rice, or create a freestyle "mosaic" by sticking on the shapes randomly.

⑦ Allow the glue to dry before lifting the picture up — you wouldn't want to ruin this masterpiece!

Note: Once the pictures are created, send them home with the kids. They do have a tendency to leave pasta pieces all over the house, even when dry, so Mom and Dad will have to deal with all that!

Clarence the Caterpillar

This accordion-like character is a lot of fun to make.

You will need:
1 piece of brightly colored 8½ x 11-inch paper
(preferably green or yellow)
poster paints and a sponge
(or easy-paint bottles with sponge tops)
glue
stick-on eyes (optional)
pipe cleaners
tape
thread or string
a straw

1. Fold your paper in half lengthwise and cut along the crease. Sponge paint each side of one half — a different color on each side — then leave to dry.

2. Fold the sponge-painted paper in half and in half again, lengthwise.

3. Open out and cut along the creases, so that you have four strips.

4. Dab some glue on the end of one strip and glue another to it, at right angles.

5. Fold the horizontal strip over the vertical strip and crease it, then fold the vertical strip over the horizontal and crease it. Continue folding alternate strips over one another to make an accordion shape.

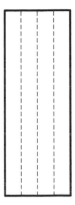

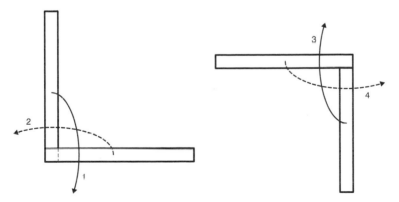

6. When you've almost finished folding the first two strips, glue the third and fourth strips onto each end of the folded strips, and continue the folding process as before.

⑦ When you've reached the end of the two strips, glue the two ends together to prevent the accordion from unraveling.

⑧ Next, choose which end will be the head and stick on the eyes (or draw/paint them on).

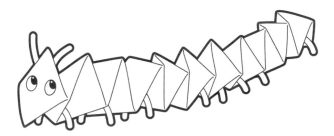

⑨ Use the pipe cleaners to make feelers and legs and attach them with tape.

⑩ Tape a piece of thread behind the head and the tail and attach the other ends to a straw so that you can make your caterpillar mobile by moving the straw up and down.

Note: You can also use this method to make a snake. Just leave the pipe cleaners off and add a forked red tongue.

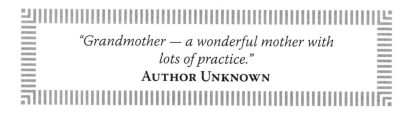

"Grandmother — a wonderful mother with lots of practice."
AUTHOR UNKNOWN

Grandmas in the Headlines

Being a grandmother doesn't mean sitting in a rocking chair and knitting all day, as these newsworthy ladies have proved.

Dancing Queen

Supple grandma Marjorie Bradbury puts women less than half her age to shame. In 2007 at the age of eighty-nine, the great-grandmother could, literally, bend over backward for her family. She could also do a split and shoulder stands, and put her legs behind her ears!

The former dance instructor from Manchester, England, studied ballet and Greek dance from a young age, and played hockey and tennis. "It's no big deal," she said modestly. "I'm sure lots of people can still do it. . . . I am not infallible."

Although she gave up her dance classes in her seventies, the spirited lady still attended regular fitness classes when the media last checked in with her in 2007.

Granny Rap

Vivian Smallwood is a California grandmother who performs hip-hop under the stage name Rappin' Granny. Born in 1933, Vivian began rapping to entertain her family after her son spotted her dancing across the room to a hip-hop beat.

After a few performances at home for her family, Vivian released a little-known, self-titled music video in 1989. Seventeen years later she hit the headlines when at the age of seventy-three she became a contestant on the hit television show *America's Got Talent.* She made it through to the finals, but lost out to eleven-year-old singer Bianca Ryan.

In addition to her rapping talents, Vivian has also appeared in a few Hollywood films and TV series, including *Everybody Hates Chris*, *The Ladykillers*, and *Malcolm in the Middle.* She now has fourteen grandchildren and five great-grandchildren.

The Karate Grandma

Bored with aerobics classes, accountant and grandmother

Mary Athay of Bristol, England, decided to take up karate. In April 2007, at the age of sixty-two, she earned a black belt. She can now break roof tiles and blocks of wood with her bare hands, but steers clear of cinder blocks in case she breaks a bone!

"It's very hard work, and getting a black belt was a huge achievement," she said. "My grandchildren think it's great fun to play-fight with me, but my husband never chats back to me now."

Inspirational Lady

A terrible accident at the height of the troubles in Northern Ireland turned Emma Groves into a world-renowned activist.

In 1971, a rubber bullet from the gun of a British soldier hit her in the face as she stood in her West Belfast, Ireland, living room. As she woke up in her hospital bed, she was greeted by Mother Teresa of Calcutta, who told her the terrible news that she had lost both her eyes. Although Emma was distressed that she would never again see the faces of her eleven children or her grandchildren, this formidable lady was spurred into action by her tragic circumstances.

Together with her friend Clara Reilly, she helped to set up the United Campaign Against Plastic Bullets, which brought together bereaved families and highlighted the issues surrounding the use of rubber and plastic bullets.

She traveled the world, campaigning and talking to political leaders, addressed the European Parliament, and led a group of families to Scotland, where they stood outside a bullet factory and informed the workers of the devastation caused by plastic bullets. She also lobbied shareholders of an American company and got them to stop manufacturing rubber bullets.

When Emma died in 2007 at the age of eighty-six, she received a host of warm tributes from her huge family, which now included forty-two grandchildren and twenty-six great-grandchildren.

"She meant everything to everybody," said granddaughter Sinead Groves. "She was the head of the family; she kept us all together. She was a party animal and enjoyed a good get-together. She was there for us all; children, grandchildren and great-grandchildren. . . . Even for the younger great-grandchildren, she was just Granny."

Senior Superstar

In 1980, after twenty years of ill health, eighty-year-old Sylvia Ginsberg of Miami was diagnosed with a heart aneurysm and told she had a maximum of one year to live. Sick of the shallow nature of celebrity culture, her grandson, essayist and short-story writer Richard Grayson, decided it was time his grandma got her fifteen minutes of fame, so he set about making it happen.

First came a press release, announcing the launch of the Sylvia Ginsberg International Fan Club, along with a magazine, which included features such as "Shocking: Why Sylvia Switched Supermarkets!," "The Untold Story of Sylvia's Artificial Hips," and "Sylvia's Love Quiz: Can *You* Pass It?"

Two days later the *Miami News* called and ran a story entitled "Grandson Fans the Flames of Stardom for Sylvia." Other journalists picked up the story, and soon Sylvia was on front pages in Los Angeles, Minneapolis, and Virginia.

As word spread, Sylvia was asked for autographs, reporters

kept knocking on her door, and neighbors started giving quotes to newspapers about what a wonderful woman she was.

Sylvia took it all in her stride, telling one newspaper that she never had a sense of humor, didn't know how to tell a joke, and wouldn't appear on *The Tonight Show* with Johnny Carson. "It's too late," she said firmly. "Who needs it? I go to bed early."

After a brief taste of the limelight, Sylvia sadly passed away — exactly one year after her diagnosis.

Record-Breaking Granny

Cathie Jung may be seventy-two, but she's no victim of middle-age spread. In fact, she's the proud owner of the smallest waist in the world.

Her tiny midriff measures just 15 inches and has landed her a place in the *Guinness World Records* book. The grandmother from Old Mystic, Connecticut, measures 39-15-39 and has been training her waist with corsets since she was forty-five. Her method has seen her shrink by 11 inches from her original 26-inch waist.

She first wore a corset when she was twenty-two, at her wedding to husband Bob, and later developed a fascination with Victorian clothing.

"I decided to start doing 'tight lacing' and wearing a corset all the time," she revealed. "My three children were grown up, so I decided to go for it. It is the time of your life when your figure begins to head south and you start to feel frumpy, so I thought it would be a good way to feel elegant and sexy."

Despite her astonishing figure, Cathie insists that she is perfectly healthy and has had X-rays to prove that the corsets have not harmed her. Luckily, her husband is an orthopedic surgeon and has confirmed that the corsets actually support the spine rather than damage it.

"Everything in the midriff is flexible," said Cathie.

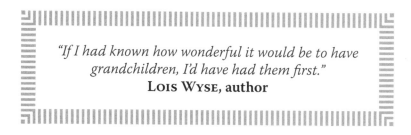

"If I had known how wonderful it would be to have grandchildren, I'd have had them first."
LOIS WYSE, author

Out on the Town with Grandma

Pedal power

With the recent resurgence in bike riding, many big parks, rural areas, and cities have safe bicycle paths for you and the children. Many will also have bikes for rent, if you don't own any yourself. These may also have seat attachments for putting babies and toddlers in while you pedal.

Make sure the smaller riders are competent on two wheels and always ensure that the whole family wears helmets. For more information about bike paths and routes in your area, contact a local bike shop or tourist information center.

Shop till they drop

The idea of taking the kids shopping may sound dull, but you can easily make it into a fun day out. If they have a birthday coming up, get them to choose their own present (within reason, of course). You can even give them a budget. That way, not only will they get something that they really want, but they will also learn a little about how much toys really cost! Getting them to hand money over and count the change is also a good way of improving their math skills.

As the children get older, they will enjoy shopping trips with you more and more (especially the girls). Treat them to a lunch out and make it an occasion. Don't let them nag you too much about buying them things, though!

Film fun

Movie tickets are surprisingly reasonable for children and those over sixty, and the multiplexes usually have something for everybody's taste.

Find out what's playing at your local theater by calling them or looking on their Web site, and then give the children a choice of what to see. Try not to choose anything too long if the children are very young, and make sure the content and rating of the film are suitable.

"Grandmas never run out of hugs or cookies."
AUTHOR UNKNOWN

If you want to keep costs down, avoid the theater's candy, popcorn, and soda, as they are generally overpriced.

Fruity fun

Fruit picking is a great day out for everyone, and there's no better way to encourage kids to eat healthy food than getting them to pick it themselves. Depending on where you live and the season, you may be able to pick strawberries, raspberries, blackberries, pumpkins, apples, pears, and even vegetables such as beans and broccoli. The hardest part is stopping the kids from eating all the fruits of their labor before you've paid for them!

To avoid disappointment, it is a good idea to call the chosen farm before you go, as weather conditions and heavy picking can affect crops and hours of business.

Teddy bears' picnic

A picnic in the park is always fun, but it can be even better for the little ones if you make it a themed event. For a teddy bears' picnic, get them to bring along one or two of their favorite bears each and make the food match the day. Sandwiches can be cut in the shape of bears, and you can find bear-shaped cookies and crackers at most supermarkets. You could include marmalade sandwiches (Paddington's favorite) or honey sandwiches (isn't it funny how bears love honey!). Take a doll's tea set if you have one, or a small cup and saucer for the bear, and involve the toys in the party.

Dolls' tea parties are an alternative, particularly if your grandchild is more into dolls than bears, and you could take the idea a few steps further with a little imagination. How about a pirate picnic, with a treasure hunt thrown in? Or a fairy picnic? Get the kids to dress up and carry the theme throughout the day.

Be advised, though, that you can end up feeling a little silly if you take it too far. It's never advisable for Grandma, whatever her age, to dance around the park in a fairy outfit!

"They say genes skip generations. Maybe that is why grandparents find their grandchildren so likeable."
JOAN MCINTOSH, poet

Silver-Haired Stars of the Silver Screen

The Blue Bird (1940)
Starring Shirley Temple

THE PLOT

Mytyl (Shirley Temple) is a spoiled, selfish girl who finds a unique bird in the Royal Forest but refuses to give it to her sick friend. That night she dreams that a fairy named Berylune sends her, along with her brother, to search for the Blue Bird of Happiness. The children have a number of adventures, including a visit with their (deceased) grandparents.

THE GRANDMA

Granny and Grandpa Tyl, played by Cecelia Loftus and Al Shean, are found in a place called the Land of the Past, where they explain, in very sweet dialogue, that they are not dead but sleeping.

"Every time you think of us, we wake up and see you again," explains Granny Tyl.

"But we thought you were dead," says Mytyl.

"No, dear," replies Granny Tyl. "Only when we're forgotten."

GOOD GRANDMA RATING

5/5 for being so sweet and touching.

On Golden Pond (1981)
Starring Katharine Hepburn, Henry Fonda, and Jane Fonda

THE PLOT
Elderly couple Ethel (Hepburn) and Norman (Fonda) Thayer are spending their summer at their house on Golden Pond when estranged daughter Chelsea (Jane Fonda) turns up with her fiancé and his thirteen-year-old son, Billy Ray. After dredging up old conflicts with her father, Chelsea leaves her parents to care for Billy Ray while she takes a trip to Europe.

THE GRANDMA
Katharine Hepburn won an Oscar for her delightful portrayal of Ethel, who provides family stability through thick and thin. She adores her husband, but is often stuck between him and their daughter. Billy Ray ends up being the catalyst that heals the rift.

GOOD GRANDMA RATING
4/5 for being a wonderful grandma and wife, although she and her daughter don't always get along.

Terms of Endearment (1983)
Starring Shirley MacLaine, Debra Winger, and Jack Nicholson

THE PLOT
The film covers three decades in the lives of Aurora Greenway (MacLaine), a fiercely protective mother, and her daughter, Emma (Winger). Disapproving of her daughter's marriage, Aurora is horrified at the prospect of becoming a grandmother. Although she grows fond of her three grandchildren, in a grudging way, she hates her son-in-law and feels vindicated when he has an affair.

THE GRANDMA
Another Oscar-winning performance in a grandmother role, this time for Shirley MacLaine. The irascible, stubborn Aurora comes through for the children when she is needed.

GOOD GRANDMA RATING
3/5 for being a fantastic character.

Peggy Sue Got Married (1986)
Starring Kathleen Turner and Nicolas Cage

THE PLOT
Peggy Sue (Turner) is a forty-three-year-old mother who is about to divorce errant husband Charlie (Cage). At her high school reunion she faints and is transported back to her teens. Faced with living her life over again, will she make the same choices?

THE GRANDMA
Veteran Hollywood star Maureen O'Sullivan appears in a small role as Elizabeth Alvorg, the grandmother Peggy gets to revisit. A touching scene has Peggy answering a phone call from her long-dead grandmother and not knowing quite what to say.

GOOD GRANDMA RATING
4/5 for playing a pivotal part in her granddaughter's life — even after her death.

Grandma's House (aka Grandmother's House) (1988)
Starring Ida Lee, Eric Foster, and Kim Valentine

THE PLOT
The movie plays on a child's fear of aloof grandmas and creepy old houses as two children, David and Lynn, are sent to live with their grandparents after the death of their father. When a dead body is found nearby, and neighbors suggest it's not the first, David and Lynn begin to suspect their dear old grandma and grandpa are serial killers.

THE GRANDMA
If your grandchildren have lost both their parents and have come to live with you, it's best not to scare the living daylights out of them. Both Grandma and Granddad are spooky as can be in this atmospheric horror movie — and that can't be good for the poor orphaned kids!

GOOD GRANDMA RATING
1/5 for taking the grandchildren in to start with.

The Princess Diaries (2001)
Starring Anne Hathaway and Julie Andrews

THE PLOT
The fifteen-year-old daughter of a single mom discovers that she is the princess of a small European principality. The death of her absent father, the crown prince of Genovia, means she is next in line to the throne. While she chooses between life as an American teenager and a role on the throne, she takes lessons in being a princess from her blue-blooded grandmother.

THE GRANDMA
Queen Clarisse Renaldi (Andrews) is well-bred and elegant, but her initial interest in her socially inept granddaughter is fueled by a desire to protect the royal bloodline. While teaching Mia (Hathaway) how to become a princess, she also learns a thing or two about family and love.

GOOD GRANDMA RATING
3/5 for final effort.

"Grandchildren don't make a woman feel old;
it's being married to a grandfather that bothers her."
AUTHOR UNKNOWN

Health Warning

One of the things to remember when your grandchildren come along is that you're not as young as you were when you had your own children. Taking care of the little darlings can be fraught with danger, so here are a few hazards to watch out for.

* New technology in the baby accessories department hasn't made strollers any easier to fold or unfold, so the likelihood of getting blistered and bleeding fingers is high. If in doubt, ask a friendly mom to help.

* Car seat buckles are notorious pinchers, and, if your two-year-old grandchild decides to arch his or her back to prevent you from fastening the buckle, you're in trouble! When in doubt, try bribery, because physically pushing him or her into the seat with one hand while fastening the three-way buckle with the other is not only painful for both of you; it's virtually impossible.

* Getting a heavy toddler in and out of the car seat can be a crunch moment — literally. Many a grandparent's back has been wrenched by this activity, and it might take weeks to recover. Take it easy and be careful how you lift.

* Young children are germ factories. The minute one child at school or day care sneezes, they are all coming down with something and, in all probability, so are you. Colds, flu, and stomach bugs are all part of being a grandma. And the annoying thing is that while the kids might shake it off in a day, it may well wipe you out for weeks.

* Lice are common in schools and day care, so if you have had contact with a lice-infested grandchild, always check your own dry hair and comb through with lots of conditioner and a fine-toothed metal comb.

* Playtime can be exhausting with young children and can also cause one or two minor injuries. Obviously, sports are good for all, but if you take to playing football or tennis in the backyard, be careful. Even more sedate play, such as jigsaw puzzles, might mean getting down on the floor. Just make sure that you can get up again!

"Always and forever is a grandmother's love."
AUTHOR UNKNOWN

Social Dangers

✳ Becoming a bore is a common mistake made by proud grandmothers. Not all your friends will appreciate a weekly viewing of thirty new photographs of little Johnny!

✳ It is also essential to remember that not everything your grandchild says or does is cute to other people. The occasional well-chosen funny story is great, but when you find yourself repeating every word your little darlings utter to a circle of fixed, polite smiles, change the subject.

✳ Be careful in the playground. You may think the lady standing next to you is another grandmother, but she could just be an older mom. Think before you speak.

✳ As desperate as you are to see your grandchildren whenever possible, you may let other hobbies and social engagements slip. Don't give up things you enjoy, as you may regret it when the family doesn't need you so much. You're not contractually obliged to say yes *every* time you're asked to babysit, and your own social life is important, too.

✳ Your bank balance may suffer. There is nothing a grandma likes more than buying little gifts for her grandchildren, but don't be tempted if you can't afford it.

✳ You stop being house-proud. After decades of keeping the home spotless and tidy, grandmas may find that they no longer care, as long as the kids are having fun. Before you know it, you'll have them drawing on the windows, splattering paint all over your best tablecloth, and kicking footballs at the flowers — all the things your own children were never allowed to do!

Story Time with Grandma

One of the loveliest activities for a grandma is reading the children a bedtime story. It's important that kids become familiar with books at an early age, and reading to them at night is a comforting, soothing routine that can calm them down before lights-out.

You don't need to spend a fortune on books, either. Second-hand stores are great places to get bargain books, or you could join the local library and have an endless free supply.

There are thousands of titles to choose from, of course, but here are a few grandparent-related stories you might like to read.

AGES 2 TO 5

Spot Visits His Grandparents by Eric Hill
  A fun lift-the-flap book about Spot the Dog's stay at his grandparents' house, where he learns more about his mom's younger days.

My Grandma Is Wonderful by Nick Butterworth
  Nick Butterworth's excellent illustrations and storytelling bring Grandma to life.

AGES 6 TO 10

George's Marvelous Medicine by Roald Dahl
  Popular children's author Roald Dahl's portrayal of George's miserable grandmother is typically dark, but very funny.

Charlie and the Chocolate Factory by Roald Dahl
  Unlike the grandma in *George's Marvelous Medicine*, the

four wacky grandparents in this wonderful tale are sweet and engaging.

A Long Way from Chicago by Richard Peck
A little more advanced (for those eight years and older), but a very amusing tale of a brother and sister's annual trip to see Grandma in her small town. Grandma Dowdel's adventures continue in ***A Year Down Yonder*** and ***A Season of Gifts***.

The *Main Street* series by Ann M. Martin
Orphaned by a car accident, sisters Flora and Ruby are adopted by their sewing-store-owning grandma, whom they call Min, in this charming series by the beloved author.

Granny Torrelli Makes Soup by Sharon Creech
A wise Italian grandmother helps a girl mend a rift with her friend over afternoons spent cooking together.

Some of the World's Greatest Grandmas

Granny Smith

We've all eaten the apple, but how many people know who the real Granny Smith was?

In fact, the juicy green fruit is named after a British lady called Maria Ann Sherwood, who was born in Peasmarsh, England, in 1799. At the age of nineteen, she married Thomas Smith, and they lived in Kent, England, until 1838, when they and several other families in the area were encouraged to emigrate to Australia, where their agricultural knowledge was in much demand.

The Smiths sailed for New South Wales, accompanied by their five children, who ranged in age from one to sixteen. Thomas found work with a wealthy Australian auctioneer in Kissing Point, Australia.

In the 1850s, Thomas bought twenty-four acres of land and set up a fruit farm that included extensive orchards. Here, Maria experimented with her own seedlings and grew new varieties of fruit.

The first account of the origin of the Granny Smith apple appeared in an article by local historian Herbert Rumsey in the *Farmer and Settler* magazine dated June 25, 1924.

In it, fruit grower Edwin Small said that, in 1868, he and his father had been invited by Maria Smith to examine a seedling on her farm that had been developed from a crab apple.

Sadly, Maria Smith didn't live to enjoy the fruits of her labor (no pun intended). She died in March 1870 before the variety became a commercial success.

Grandma Moses

Grandma Moses became one of America's most celebrated artists after taking up painting in her seventies. The hardworking farmer's wife and mother of ten started life as Anna Mary Robertson in September 1860. As a child she drew on wood, using fruit juice as paint, and when her father bought candy for her nine siblings, Anna would receive the drawing supplies she preferred.

She married Thomas Solomon Moses in 1887, and in 1905 they settled on a farm in Eagle Bridge, New York. When a doctor told her to stop working on the farm because of her arthritis and neuritis, the grandmother of eleven turned to embroidery and then painting "to keep busy and out of mischief."

In 1938, when she was seventy-eight, Grandma Moses's pictures caught the eye of an art collector who saw them hanging in her local drugstore. A year later a hugely successful exhibition of her work was hosted in New York and word spread throughout the country. She was featured on radio, on television, and in magazines, and became an overnight sensation.

In a 1948 interview with *Time* magazine, Anna, by then a great-grandmother of ten, said, "When I had my children and grandchildren, I was about as busy as they were. I never had much good of them. I have more time now for my great-grandchildren."

Nonetheless, she continued to paint her hugely popular rural scenes and exhibited them throughout America, Europe, and Japan. At the age of one hundred, she illustrated Clement Moore's now-classic rhyming text *A Visit from St. Nicholas* (otherwise known as *'Twas the Night Before Christmas*).

Grandma Moses outlived all her children and, when she died at the age of 101, she was survived by her daughter-in-law Dorothy, nine grandchildren, and more than thirty great-grandchildren.

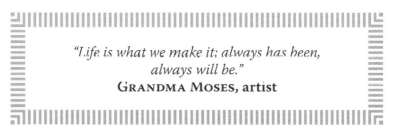

"Life is what we make it; always has been, always will be."
GRANDMA MOSES, artist

Queen Victoria

A formidable lady, Queen Victoria became known as the "grandmother of Europe" after many of her children and grandchildren married into the royal families of other European countries.

She ascended to the British throne in 1837 at the age of eighteen. Three years later she married her first cousin, Prince Albert of Saxe-Coburg-Gotha, and in the following years she had nine children, all of whom survived to adulthood, which was rare at the time.

The death of her beloved husband in 1861 threw Queen Victoria into a period of deep mourning that was to last ten years. Even after she retuned to public life, she always dressed in black and, when she died in 1901, she was buried with a portrait of her prince beside her.

Although in her austere mourning dresses Queen Victoria may have seemed a frightening sight to small children, she was a warm and loving person who put great stock in family.

A grandmother at thirty-nine and a great-grandmother twenty years later, Queen Victoria was proud of her youthful looks and wrote to her daughter, "I own it seems funny to me to be a grandmamma and so many people tell me they can't believe it!"

Although she didn't see much of her European family, she was an adoring grandmother and great-grandmother when she could spend time with them.

Christmas was a joyous occasion for Victoria until the death of her beloved Albert, and it remained a family occasion even throughout her mourning. The Queen always spent the day at Osborne House on the Isle of Wight, surrounded by children, grandchildren, and, in her later years, great-grandchildren.

On the birth of grandson George, later King George V, she

asked that he be called Frederick, but gave in to his parents' preference. "If the dear child grows up good and wise," she wrote, "I shall not mind what his name is."

Queen Elizabeth, the Queen Mother

Children can often feel closer to their grandparents than to their own parents, and the Queen Mother was certainly a huge influence on Prince Charles throughout his life.

Her first grandchild, Charles was very precious to the Queen Mother, and when his mother, Queen Elizabeth II, was too busy with official duties, he turned to his grandmother for solace and guidance.

The Queen and the Duke of Edinburgh were often away on state visits abroad, and it was during these absences that Charles and his sister, Anne, grew close to the Queen Mother. When he went to boarding school, it was she to whom Charles turned to voice his unhappiness.

They shared a similar sense of humor and a special understanding. Royal biographer Anthony Holden said, "More than either of Charles's parents, perhaps, his grandmother understood the ordeal of the quiet, uncertain child in a harsh and alien world."

Born Elizabeth Bowes-Lyon in August 1900, she married Albert, Duke of York, in 1923 and had two children, Elizabeth and Margaret. Her world was turned upside down in 1936 when King Edward VIII abruptly abdicated to marry his mistress, Wallis Simpson, and Elizabeth's husband, who was next in line to the throne, became king.

It was a task that she believed detrimental to "Bertie's" health, and she never forgave her brother-in-law for thrusting it upon him. But if Bertie, now known as King George VI, suffered, the Queen's own indomitable spirit shone through.

During World War II she gained the love of the nation by refusing to leave London and by visiting bombed-out communities to offer moral support. Her actions raised morale so much that Adolf Hitler called her "the most dangerous woman in Europe."

Widowed in 1952, she became the family matriarch when Queen Mary died a year later, and she remained the most beloved member of the royal family until her death in 2002.

The Prince of Wales called her "one of the most remarkable and wonderful people in the world," and shortly after her death he said he missed her "more than I can possibly say."

As well as being a real grandmother to six, the Queen Mother held such a place in the hearts of the British people that she became known as "grandmother of the nation."

> *"The children will not leave unless I do. I shall not leave unless their father does, and the King will not leave the country in any circumstances whatever."*
> **QUEEN ELIZABETH, THE QUEEN MOTHER,**
> refusing to leave London during World War II

Margaret Thatcher, Baroness

When Margaret Thatcher's first grandchild, Michael, was born, Britain's first and only female prime minister famously announced her new status with the line, "We have become a grandmother."

Using the "royal we," previously reserved for the monarch, led to much ridicule and some suggestions that power had gone to her head, but the moment also showed that even one as tough as the Iron Lady could be touched by the unique moment of becoming a grandma for the first time.

"If you want anything said, ask a man.
If you want something done, ask a woman."
MARGARET THATCHER, former British prime minister

Born Margaret Hilda Roberts in 1925, the daughter of a grocer, she married Denis Thatcher in 1951 and became a lawyer in 1953, the same year her twins, Carol and Mark, were born. After becoming a member of Parliament six years later, she rose through the ranks of the Conservative Party to become its leader in 1975. A landslide election in 1979 was the start of an eleven-year term as prime minister, the longest ever served in the United Kingdom.

The core values at the root of her Conservative ideals she attributed to her grandmother. "I was brought up by a Victorian grandmother," she said. "We were taught to work jolly hard. We were taught to prove yourself; we were taught self-reliance; we were taught to live within our income.

"You were taught that cleanliness is next to godliness. You were taught self-respect. You were taught always to give a hand to your neighbor. You were taught tremendous pride in your country. All of these things are Victorian values. They are also perennial values. You don't hear so much about these things these days, but they were good values and they led to tremendous improvements in the standard of living."

Teenagers Revisited

There will come a time when your gorgeous, cute, and clever grandchild turns into a grumpy, hormone-filled monster. You might remember that a similar thing happened to your own sweet children!

If you're lucky, all the sarcasm and anger will be directed at their parents and you'll get off scot-free. But don't be surprised if you are no longer their favorite person and they are more interested in going to see their friends than in visiting Grandma.

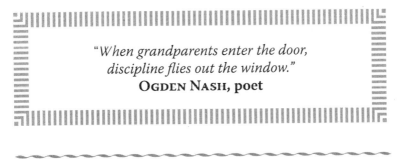

"When grandparents enter the door,
discipline flies out the window."
OGDEN NASH, poet

How to Get Through to Your Teenage Grandchildren

DO:

Take a computer class

New technology is not only for the young. Silver-haired surfers are all the rage, and there's no better way to surprise your teenage grandchildren than by knowing more about computers than they do.

Take an interest in their interests

Whether it's drama, sports, or reading books, find out about the subject and bring it up. If they are fans of a football team, find out the names of the players and keep track of how they are doing.

Treat them as grown-ups

One of the biggest frustrations of being a teenager is that you don't feel like a child, but nobody treats you as an adult. Suggest grown-up activities like playing board and card games, and take them to restaurants and cafés rather than a family-style restaurant.

Start each conversation with an open question

If a question requires a yes or no answer, chances are that's what you'll get — with attitude. Instead, try asking questions that require a sentence reply, such as "What have you been doing today?" or "What do you have planned for the weekend?"

Keep up with showbiz gossip

Surf the net or buy the occasional celebrity magazine. That way you might occasionally know what on earth they're talking about!

DON'T:

Start every sentence with "When I was a girl . . ."

Reliving the good old days may be one of the joys of getting older, but teenagers are easily bored. Keep your nostalgia to yourself, except for a few select stories from time to time.

Buy (or download) the same music as they

It's one thing to know whom they're talking about, but it's another to be rushing out to buy the latest rap album to impress them. They won't be impressed — they'll be embarrassed!

Embarrass them in public

They may be your best friend when they are alone with you, but when they are with their own friends, keep your distance. If you see them on the street, say hello, but don't make a big fuss, and *never* baby them.

Play the tough parent

They get enough of that at home! If teenage moodiness is causing problems with their parents, your company should be a safe haven from all the arguments.

Take sides

If your teenage grandchild has had a fight with Mom, don't add to his or her anguish by saying, "Your mom's right!" Nor should you side with your grandchild. Stay out of it.

Things You Should Never Say to a Teenager

"When I was your age, I was already working."

"Ooh, your skin looks terrible today."

"There are plenty more fish in the sea."

"Since your mom's away, you can come home anytime you like."

"That's a lovely miniskirt. May I borrow it?"

"Of course you can borrow my cell phone."

"The youth of today have no manners."

"You look really cute in that outfit."

You Know You're a Grandma When . . .

* You start saying "Bless him" all the time.

* You find the slightest excuse to call your children.

* You walk past the designer dresses and head for the children's department at your favorite clothing store.

* Your children suddenly want to see a lot more of you.

* The most exciting event on your calendar is a toddler's birthday party.

* You can't pass a toy store without buying something.

* You get competitive about a baby's ability to walk or talk.

* You actually look forward to changing diapers.

* You are immune to crying, whining, and tantrums and see only sweetness.

* Your house resembles a bomb site for the first time in years, and you don't care!

Long-Distance Grandma

Grandmas are not always on the doorstep, and it can be heart-breaking to be too far from your grandchildren to see them on a regular basis. But that doesn't mean you can't be a big part of their lives.

Here are a few tips for long-distance grandmas.

Use snail mail

In the days of telephones, text messages, and e-mails, children rarely receive real letters. As a consequence, they love to get something through the mail, whether it is a letter,

a postcard, or a small package. Don't compensate for your absence by sending expensive gifts — a simple letter or a card telling them your news will be just as exciting for them.

Send photos

Your children will undoubtedly send you regular photos of the grandkids so that you can keep up to date, but it should be a two-way street. Granted your looks won't change on a regular basis, but if you go somewhere exciting and a photo is taken, send one to your grandchildren with a little note about the event.

Plan visits well

For your sake, and those of the child's parents, make sure you plan your trips well in advance. Always discuss with the parents when you will come and when you will be leaving, so there are no surprises. If it is a long stay, plan days out with the children and give their parents some space.

Tell the children what you have planned

Send a letter, call, or e-mail and tell the grandkids what fun days lie ahead. They will love looking forward to your visit. But

> *"An hour with your grandchildren can make you feel young again. Anything longer than that, and you start to age quickly."*
> **GENE PERRET, comedy writer**

be careful — never promise a child something that you can't deliver. If something is weather dependent, for example, don't make any pledges until you know what the day will be like.

Offer to babysit

If you are staying more than a night or two, suggest that your son or daughter and partner take the opportunity to go out alone. If it is a long visit, and they feel they must spend every evening entertaining you, it may make life stressful. An evening out for them will break up the visit and give you time alone with the grandchildren.

Help out — to a point

Some mothers complain that their mother-in-law never lifts a finger, while others moan that she does too much and interferes in housework routines and cooking. Try to strike a happy medium. Offer to prepare dinner, set the table, or do the dishes, but don't be too pushy. You may be just as useful if you are keeping the kids occupied while Mom or Dad takes care of routine domestic activities.

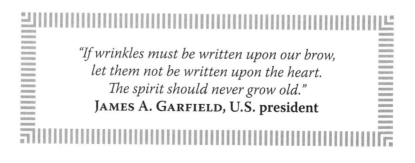

"If wrinkles must be written upon our brow,
let them not be written upon the heart.
The spirit should never grow old."
JAMES A. GARFIELD, U.S. president

The Other Woman

If your grandchildren are lucky enough to have two grand-mothers, you will need to handle your rival carefully. Whatever your previous relationship with your child's mother-in-law, jealousy is about to rear its ugly head in a way you wouldn't think possible.

After all, your children had only one mom, so there was no real rival for their affection. Now you have fallen in love all

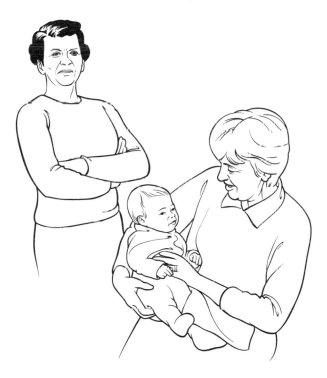

over again, and every moment your beloved grandchild spends with the other grandma may make you feel like a jealous teenager whose first crush is eyeing another girl!

Here are a few tips on handling the situation with as much dignity as possible.

* Whatever your relationship with the other grandmother before your grandchild was born, don't let that change. If you were great friends beforehand and spent time together, continue to do so, but don't bring baby along, too. That will only complicate matters.

* If you rarely socialized before, don't let your children strong-arm you into big get-togethers unless you are comfortable sharing your family with the in-laws at such an event.

* If you do attend a social gathering together, be careful not to hog the grandchildren, as this will cause resentment.

* If your grandchildren are determined to spend all their time with you — you are the fun grandma, after all — do the right thing. Discreetly suggest that they go and talk to grandma number two or steer them in her direction if they want help with a picture or a game.

* Conversation at such events should not revolve around the kids. You may like to swap stories, but don't let it turn into a competition. If it is heading that way, talk about something else.

* Never gloat! If you have a bigger backyard, can afford more expensive gifts, or have more time for day trips, there's no need to rub it in.

* Inevitably, the other grandmother will have different ideas and ways of doing things. She may be more of a

disciplinarian, or you may feel she spoils the children. Either way, she loves them as much as you do. *Never* criticize her in front of the kids.

✳ If your child or his or her partner moans about the other grandmother, don't be tempted to join in. Remember that harsh words could come back to bite you. Whatever the other grandma has done to upset your brood, it is not your argument, so stay out of it.

✳ Accept her talents. The other grandma may be a better cook, excellent at making things, or fantastic at music. Don't compete in the same field, but find things you are good at and make it fun for the kids.

✳ Babysitting time should never become a competition. If geography, family closeness, or just busy lives mean that you get to see less of the little ones than their other grandparents, accept it. It might hurt, but you should make the most of the time spent with them rather than worrying about the time that someone else is spending with them.

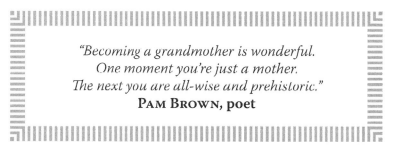

"Becoming a grandmother is wonderful.
One moment you're just a mother.
The next you are all-wise and prehistoric."
PAM BROWN, poet

✳ Research has shown that a child's maternal grandmother is likely to be the closest to the family, as daughters often turn to their mothers for help and advice, and tend to be closer to their moms than sons. This means that if you are the paternal grandma, you may have to take a backseat and accept that your co-grandma has more influence on the children's upbringing.

❋ If you feel you are not seeing enough of the children, don't start a fight or compare yourself to the other grandma. Suggest your son or daughter might like a day off or a night out and ask to babysit. Few busy parents would turn that offer down!

The Imperfect Parents

Remember that the arrival of a baby, particularly the first one, can put a strain on the best of relationships. Your son or daughter and his or her partner have a lot of adjusting to do, and your behavior could be a help or a hindrance.

Whatever you thought of your son-in-law or daughter-in-law before, he or she is now the parent of your grandchild and needs your support and encouragement — not a sniping, over-bearing mother-in-law.

Here are a few things to keep in mind.

✳ If you are the maternal grandmother and spend a lot of time with your daughter and the children, be sure you don't make Dad feel left out. He may feel that he is being ganged up on, which won't help your daughter's relationship at all.

✳ Dads today are very different from what they were thirty years ago. Dad is as likely to be changing the diapers and getting up in the night as Mom is, so don't assume he knows nothing about child rearing.

✳ If it is your son's baby who is the latest addition to the family, tread carefully. Remember how you were with your babies. A new mother has the instinct of a lioness and can be just as fierce if crossed. She may take endless advice from her own mother, but that doesn't mean she'll appreciate yours!

✳ Never criticize your children's partners. Just as they will defend you if you are being maligned, they will defend their partners rather than admit any faults.

✳ Stay out of family arguments. Your daughter may be on the phone in tears, telling you how mean her husband is, but you should never take sides. Chances are the next day they'll be back in each other's arms, and negative comments from you could come back to haunt you.

✳ Always follow the parents' lead on important issues such as religion, manners, and moral behavior. You may not like the fact that your grandchild is being brought up with different values, but that is his or her parents' choice.

* Do praise the parenting skills of your child and his or her partner. No parent is ever sure he or she is doing everything right, and grandparents are all too quick to criticize. How many people say, "You're a wonderful mom," or "You're a great dad"? It can mean the world to a stressed parent.

* Praise the children to their parents, too. No mom or dad ever tires of hearing how smart, talented, kind, or polite his or her children are.

* Don't compare one set of grandchildren with their cousins. Much as your offspring may love their nieces and nephews, they don't want to keep hearing how wonderful they are.

* Avoid a showdown. If things are building up to the point where you may say something you'll regret, take a deep breath and step back.

* Learn how to apologize. If an issue does come up and harsh words are exchanged, there is no joy in standing your ground if it means losing your children and grandchildren. Pride will be no comfort then.

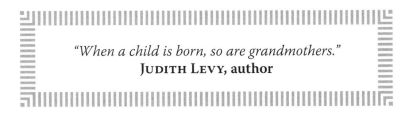

"When a child is born, so are grandmothers."
JUDITH LEVY, author

Grandma's Words of Wisdom

Grandmothers have always been prone to producing an old wives' tale for every occasion. But are they talking nonsense or revealing pearls of wisdom that make perfect sense?

Toast always lands butter side down

This is true in more than 90 percent of cases, and the reason is not just Murphy's Law, as you might think. It is largely due to the height of the average kitchen counter from which most slices of toast are dropped. The toast, which usually falls at an angle, rotates as it descends because of its uneven weight, which is caused by the butter. Because of the height it drops from, it rotates only halfway before hitting the floor. If dropped from twice the height, it would, in most cases, rotate the full 360 degrees and land butter side up.

Chocolate gives you pimples

This assertion, long spouted by parents and grandparents to troubled teenagers with devastating acne, is a myth. Acne is caused by overproduction of oil that causes a partial blockage of a pore. Because this is influenced by hormones, it is more prevalent in teenagers. Many studies have examined the relationship between diet and acne, and none has ever found any conclusive evidence to support a link between chocolate or fried foods and pimples.

Cheese gives you nightmares

Grandma is proven wrong on this one. Recent research has shown that vitamin B_6, found in large quantities in cheese, actually helps you to sleep. Studies found that insomnia sufferers were often lacking in serotonin. In order to make more serotonin, the body requires vitamin B_6, which is found in cheese, carrots, fish, lentils, peas, potatoes, sunflower seeds, and whole grain flour. So if you have sleepless nights, up your intake of these foods, and ignore Grandma's nightmare warning.

Cats always land on their feet

A cat's ability to fall from a great height and walk away unscathed has fueled the myth that the animal has nine lives. Research conducted in 1987 by two New York vets, who studied animals brought to them after falls of between two and thirty-two stories, discovered that the most injuries were caused by falls from around seven stories. Falls from heights above that, bizarrely, caused fewer injuries. The reason the cats fared so well in general was because of a high surface-area-to-mass ratio, which means a lower velocity is reached. They are also more flexible and can twist midflight to land on their feet, absorbing the shock through the soft tissue of their legs. The seventh story is thought to be the height that enables cats to reach their terminal velocity before hitting the ground. As they accelerate, they stiffen up with fright. After terminal velocity is reached, they are no longer accelerating and appear to relax, which explains why cats falling from higher stories sustained fewer injuries.

A word of caution: It is not advisable to test this theory by throwing your pet out the window of a high-rise building.

> *"God couldn't be everywhere,*
> *so he created grandmothers."*
> **AUTHOR UNKNOWN**

Black makes you look slimmer

This is the real reason that black never goes out of fashion. Black clothing works because we perceive shapes by the shadows and shades we see. These are not visible on black and, therefore, the shape appears more flat. Wearing black is a great way to hide those lumps and bumps.

A silver spoon in the neck of an open Champagne bottle retains the fizz

Some believe it is a stainless steel spoon but, in fact, this appears to be a myth. Winemaker Frédéric Panaïotis, of Veuve Clicquot, has revealed the results of an experiment conducted by the company that tested 180 open bottles of Champagne. Some had a silver spoon inserted into the neck, some stainless steel spoons, and some had none at all. The next day there was some fizz in all the bottles, but the spoon made no difference at all. Frédéric added, "In all the bottles there was some oxidization, which you want to avoid. The best thing is to drink it all at once."

Red sky at night, sailors' delight;
Red sky in morning, sailors' warning

This old wives' tale does have some foundation in truth, but only in midlatitude locations. Clouds often appear red in the morning and evening because of the way the spectrum of colors breaks up as light passes through the atmosphere. At sunrise and sunset the light has farther to travel than at other times, and red is able to travel farther than the other colors without being diverted and is then reflected off the clouds. In midlatitude locations, winds are westerly, and the sun rises in the east and sets in the west. This means red sky at night indicates that the clouds are in the east, and therefore are being blown away. A red sky in the morning means the clouds are in the west, and heading toward you.

You can't get one cold right after another

You certainly can. Actually, unless you take care of yourself very well during a brief illness, you are more likely to catch another cold. The increased resistance you gain from being ill works only on exactly the same strain of the virus, and the common cold comes in more than two hundred varieties.

Eat shellfish only when there is an "r" in the name of the month

When people used to gather their own shellfish, this was excellent advice, as toxic algae that affected the shellfish could multiply in summer — months without the "r." These days it's safe to eat shellfish all year round due to modern harvesting methods and improved hygiene regulations.

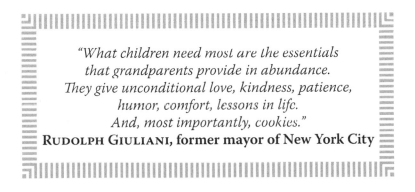

"What children need most are the essentials
that grandparents provide in abundance.
They give unconditional love, kindness, patience,
humor, comfort, lessons in life.
And, most importantly, cookies."
RUDOLPH GIULIANI, former mayor of New York City

Laughter is the best medicine

Grandma is right on this one. Studies show that laughter boosts levels of endorphins, the body's natural painkillers, and decreases levels of epinephrine, the stress hormone.

A study at the University of Maryland Medical Center in Baltimore also concluded that a good chuckle on a regular basis can lower the risk of heart disease and, by association, heart attack. So a laugh a day just might keep the doctor away.

Household Tips

Your years of experience around the house mean that daughters and sons may often ask you for advice. But if your idea of household hints is no more complicated than picking up the latest cleaning product from the local supermarket, your grandma credentials need a boost. Here are a few traditional tips to pass on.

Lemon juice prevents a cut apple from browning

When an apple is cut, its cells leak phenolic compounds, which mix with the apple's enzymes and are then oxidized by contact with the air, turning the apple brown. Lemon juice contains the antioxidant vitamin C, which is clear when oxidized and prevents the phenolic chemicals from causing any browning.

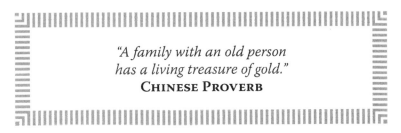

"A family with an old person has a living treasure of gold."
CHINESE PROVERB

Add a drop of vinegar to pans

When boiling eggs, add a little vinegar to the pan to avoid leaving any white watermarks.

Remove lime scale marks with vinegar

If your bath or sink has a buildup of lime scale, soak some cloths and rags in white vinegar, cover the marks, and leave the rags to soak overnight.

Add water to a grill pan

Before grilling greasy food, half fill the grill pan with water. When you have finished with the grill, dispose of the remaining water and wipe the grill pan with a damp cloth and a little liquid dishwashing soap.

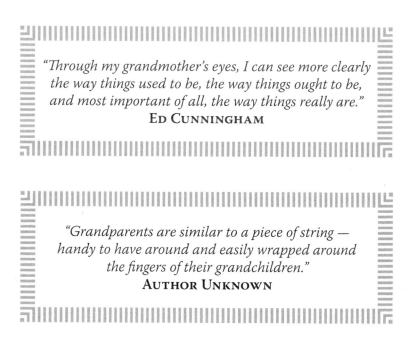

"Through my grandmother's eyes, I can see more clearly the way things used to be, the way things ought to be, and most important of all, the way things really are."
ED CUNNINGHAM

"Grandparents are similar to a piece of string — handy to have around and easily wrapped around the fingers of their grandchildren."
AUTHOR UNKNOWN

Cleaning up a broken egg

If you drop an egg on the floor, pour salt over it and leave it for a few minutes. The egg will harden and will be much easier to clean up.

Cleaning odors and grease from a carpet

Pour baking soda over grease spots and brush through the pile of the rug. Leave overnight, then vacuum gently.

Preventing pollen stains

If you are lucky enough to be given a bouquet with flowers prone to dropping pollen, such as lilies, take a piece of damp paper towel and gently wipe the pollen from each stamen.

Removing chewing gum

To remove chewing gum from fabric and carpets, freeze the gum with an ice cube to harden it before scraping it off with a knife or pinching it clean with your fingers. Then pretreat and gently wash the fabric or carpet.

A Song for Grandma

From the memorable number-one hit "There's No One Quite Like Grandma" to the quirky Christmas tune "Grandma Got Run Over by a Reindeer," grandmothers of all kinds have been immortalized in a number of eclectic songs.

❋ "Granny's Song" — SHEILA KAY ADAMS

❋ "Grandma's Hands" — BILL WITHERS

❋ "Grandmother's Song" — STEVE MARTIN

❋ "Grandma" — MIKE JONES

❋ "Grandma Told Grandpa" — LIGHTNIN' HOPKINS

❋ "Hey Grandma" — MOBY GRAPE

❋ "Grandma's Feather Bed" — JOHN DENVER

❋ "Grandma Got Run Over by a Reindeer" — ELMO & PATSY

❋ "Granny" — DAVE MATTHEWS BAND

❋ "Grandma's Party" — PAUL NICHOLAS

❋ "A Song for Grandma and Grandpa" — JOHNNY PRILL

It's Never Too Late To . . .

Become a rock star

In May 2007, a group of forty British retirees came together to become singing sensation The Zimmers, a pop group with a combined age of more than three thousand years.

Their first single was a cover of The Who's "My Generation," which they recorded at the famous Abbey Road Studios in London. The video of the recording, posted on YouTube, received 1.5 million hits in just two weeks, and the song itself reached number twenty-six on the British pop charts.

Three members of the group also embarked on a publicity tour to Los Angeles, and appeared on *The Tonight Show* with Jay Leno, alongside movie star George Clooney.

* * *

Set up a blog

María Amelia López was a Spanish grandmother who called herself "the world's oldest blogger." When her grandson, Daniel, set up her Internet blog in December 2006 — a present for her ninety-fifth birthday — she began updating it regularly.

Nicknamed "the little granny" by her readers, she dictated her entries to Daniel and used her blog to describe aspects of her life. She also offered many insightful thoughts on modern life to her readers. "It's like having a conversation," she once said. "Those who read what I say become my friends." Sadly, López died in May 2009 at the age of ninety-seven.

The Joke's on Grandma

After playing outside with some friends, little Johnny came indoors to ask his grandma a puzzling question.

"Grandma," he said. "What is it called when two people are sleeping in the same room and one is on top of the other?"

A little shocked, his granny replied, "It's called sexual intercourse."

Satisfied with her answer, Johnny went back to playing with his friends. Minutes later, he stormed back into the house with a tear-stained face.

"Grandma, it is not called sexual intercourse!" he cried. "It's called bunk beds, and Jimmy's mom wants to talk to you!"

✳ ✳ ✳

A young boy and his doting grandmother were walking on the beach when a huge wave appeared out of nowhere, sweeping the child out to sea. The horrified woman fell to her knees and started praying.

"Lord, return my grandson to me and I will be eternally grateful," she wailed.

As she prayed, another huge wave built up and deposited the terrified child on the sand, at which Grandma stared angrily toward the heavens and remarked, "When we came, my grandson had a hat!"

* * *

A hospital receptionist picked up the phone to the voice of a sweet old grandma.

"Could I get some information on a patient, please?" the woman asked.

"Yes, of course," replied the receptionist. "What's the name and room number?"

"Lucy Mayes, room twenty-two," said the old lady.

"I'll just check her chart," the girl replied. "Oh, good news. She's doing very well, making a speedy recovery, and the doctor says she can go home on Wednesday. Are you a relative?"

"No," answered the grandma. "*I'm* Lucy Mayes in room twenty-two. Nobody tells me anything!"

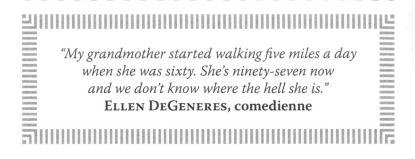

"My grandmother started walking five miles a day when she was sixty. She's ninety-seven now and we don't know where the hell she is."
ELLEN DEGENERES, comedienne

The following account has been reported as a true story, but it just might be an urban myth.

Returning from a shopping trip, an elderly lady found four men about to drive off in her car. She dropped her shopping bags and pulled out a gun, then screamed at the top of her voice, "I have a gun and I know how to use it — get out of the car, you scumbags!"

The men jumped out of the car and ran for their lives, while the old woman loaded her bags and got into the driver's seat.

Still shaken by the incident, she had trouble getting the key into the ignition and, after a few tries, she suddenly realized why. A few minutes later she found her own car parked four or five spaces away!

Horrified at her terrible mistake, she drove to the police station and confessed all. The officer laughed and pointed to the other end of the counter. There stood four pale, shaken men who were reporting a carjacking by a crazy elderly woman described as less than five feet tall with curly white hair, who was wearing glasses and carrying a large handgun.

No charges were filed.

✳ ✳ ✳

One day, a ninety-five-year-old widow decided she was ready to join her late husband in heaven.

After finding his old army pistol, she decided the quickest way would be to shoot herself through the heart. Determined to make sure she got it right the first time, she called her doctor and asked exactly where she would find her heart.

"It's just below your left breast," the helpful doctor informed her.

Later that night, she was admitted to the hospital with a gunshot wound to her knee.

✳ ✳ ✳

When little Michael's grandma came to visit, he ran up and gave her a big hug.

"I'm so happy to see you, Grandma," he said excitedly. "Now Daddy will have to do that trick he's been promising to do!"

"What trick is that, darling?" asked his grandmother, intrigued.

"I heard Daddy tell Mommy that he would climb the walls if you came to stay with us again!"

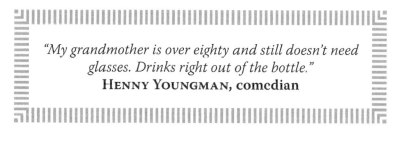

"My grandmother is over eighty and still doesn't need glasses. Drinks right out of the bottle."
HENNY YOUNGMAN, comedian

Also available in this bestselling series: